First Steps in Mathematica

Werner Burkhardt

First Steps in
Mathematica

Springer-Verlag
London Berlin Heidelberg New York
Paris Tokyo Hong Kong
Barcelona Budapest

Werner Burkhardt
Talstrasse 42
68259 Mannheim
Germany

ISBN 3-540-19875-X Springer-Verlag Berlin Heidelberg New York
ISBN 0-387-19875-X Springer-Verlag New York Berlin Heidelberg

Originally published in German under the title: Erste Schritte mit Mathematica
Copyright © Springer-Verlag Berlin Heidelberg 1993.
All Rights Reserved.

Translation by M. J. Stewart

British Library Cataloguing in Publication Data
A catalogue record for this book is available from the British Library

Library of Congress Cataloging-in-Publication Data
A catalog record for this book is available from the Library of Congress

© Springer-Verlag London Limited 1994

The use of registered names, trademarks etc. in this publication does not imply, even in the absence of a specific statement, that such names are exempt from the relevant laws and regulations and therefore free for general use.

The publisher makes no representations, express or implied, with regard to the accuracy of the information contained in this book and cannot accept any legal responsibility or liability for any errors or omissions that may be made.

Typeset by Richard Powell Editorial and Production Services,
Basingstoke RG22 4TX
Printed by Athenæum Press Ltd, Gateshead, England
34/3830-54321 (printed on acid-free paper)

Contents

Preface . . . . *vii*

1	**Introduction**	**1**
1.1	Starting *Mathematica*	1
1.2	Calculating with numbers	3
1.3	Calculating with real numbers and functions	6
1.4	Calculating with complex numbers and functions . . .	6
1.5	Problems	11
2	**Term transformations**	**12**
2.1	Calculating with symbols	12
2.2	Calculating with rational integral terms	14
2.3	Calculating with fractions (rational expressions)	18
2.4	Problems	20
3	**Lists, tables and functions**	**21**
3.1	Lists	21
3.2	Tables	23
3.3	Functions	24
3.4	Problems	26
4	**Solution of equations**	**27**
4.1	Solution of rational integral equations	27
4.2	Equations with square roots and absolute values . . .	31
4.3	Trigonometric equations	33
4.4	Problems	37
5	**Linear algebra and sets of equations**	**38**
5.1	Description of matrices and vectors	38
5.2	Transformation matrices	40
5.3	Calculating with vectors	43
5.4	Solution of systems of equations	44
5.5	Problems	47
6	**Graphics**	**48**
6.1	2D graphics	48
6.2	3D graphics	55
6.3	Problems	62

7	**Analysis**	**63**
7.1	Derivatives	63
7.2	Integrals	66
7.3	Limits, series and products	68
7.4	Differential equations	71
7.5	Problems	74
8	**Simple programs**	**76**
8.1	Rule-based programs	76
8.2	Altering commands	78
8.3	Procedural programs	79
Appendix A	**Installation on PCs**	**82**
A.1	Installation under MS-DOS	82
A.2	Installation under MS-Windows	85
Appendix B	**List of commands**	**87**
Appendix C	**Solutions**	**94**
C.1	Solutions to Chapter 1	94
C.2	Solutions to Chapter 2	94
C.3	Solutions to Chapter 3	95
C.4	Solutions to Chapter 4	95
C.5	Solutions to Chapter 5	95
C.6	Solutions to Chapter 6	96
C.7	Solutions to Chapter 7	96
References		*97*
Index		*98*

Preface

Before the age of computers – that is, before 1950 – a mathematical calculation involved a mixture of numerical and analytical manipulations. To quote a somewhat extreme example, the moonbeam calculations made by Delaunay in the last century show how this procedure could be very time-consuming: he took 10 years to produce his calculations, and a further 10 years to check them!

Few of us can afford such single-minded – not to say long-winded – dedication to a problem in the computer age of the 1990s. The widespread availability of computer systems means that many problems can be prepared numerically and then worked out by machine, and results obtained vastly more quickly than by the older methods. As a result of the success of such an approach many scientists today regard the concepts of numerical calculation and scientific calculation as synonymous.

Unfortunately, however, this method has disadvantages:

- Rounding errors affect the results.
- Problems that are analytically exactly solvable are only solved approximately by numerical methods. Thus the structure of the numerical solution is often not clearly recognisable.

Because of these disadvantages, attempts were made to reconstruct on computers the pencil and paper methods used by everyone before the introduction of computers. The first attempts are to be found in the work of Kahrimanian and Nolen, who in 1953 published an article on symbolic differentiation in computer systems. In the 1960s some computer algebraic systems were developed for mainframes. At the end of the 1970s the first computer algebraic systems for PCs appeared; these were criticised by some for requiring as much time as paper calculations, even though they lightened the burden of calculation! This was largely because of the need to learn the system's programming language and interpret the results. Fortunately, with the increasing power and productivity of PCs it became possible to implement more user-friendly computer algebraic systems on PCs. *Mathematica* is one of these systems, and its development goes back to 1980.

Stephen Wolfram began with the development of the rule-based programming language SMP as a crystallisation of his work on cellular automata. This program was the precursor of *Mathematica*. The results of this work were introduced into many scientific disciplines (biology, physics, chaos research, etc.). Wolfram's further research into complex systems and the physics of flow led in 1986 to the founding of Wolfram Research Inc., with the aim of developing *Mathematica* further. In June 1988 Version 1.0 of *Mathematica* for the Apple Macintosh first appeared, to be followed by versions for other machines. The list now includes: Convex, DEC VAX (Ultrix and VMS) and RISC, Hewlett-Packard/Apollo, IBM 386-PCs and compatibles under MS-DOS or MS Windows, IBM RISC, MIPS, NeXT, Silicon Graphics, Sony and Sun, as well as mainframes. This selection is certainly not complete, because the number of platforms for which *Mathematica* is being made available is constantly growing. At the time of writing, the currently available version is 2.1, although the next version has already been announced.

This book contains an introduction to *Mathematica* that provides all the basic knowledge required to use the package. This knowledge is conveyed by means of examples based on numerous questions from school and college mathematics; at the end of each chapter problems are included to test the reader's knowledge (solutions are given at the end of the book). I have made a point of choosing examples that are:

- Relevant to applications
- Illustrative of the capabilities (and limitations) of *Mathematica*

Because of this choice of examples the book is especially suitable for the following readership:

- Self-study users of computer algebraic systems
- Those taking courses in *Mathematica* in schools and colleges
- Those receiving scientific mathematical instruction at university level

In conclusion I should like to thank Mr J. Lammarsch for his stimulation and encouragement to write this book. My thanks too to Mrs Luzia Dietsche of DANTE e.V., to whom I frequently took my questions about LATEX, and who always helped me on my way. Finally, I should like to thank my family, who showed such understanding during the time that I was preoccupied with this book.

Werner Burkhardt

1 Introduction

In common with many other computer-based algebra systems that are designed as input/output systems, *Mathematica* accepts a task (input) and provides the solution (output). To ensure that it can be used on many different computers, two basic principles were followed in writing the *Mathematica* software:

1. The kernel is the same for all computers.
2. The front end depends on the type of machine.

Currently, both text- and graphics-oriented user interfaces (notebooks) are obtainable. Since it would be beyond the scope of this book to describe all of these in full, we shall restrict ourselves to describing only the input techniques that are possible with all systems. The inputs and outputs are shown in a `typewriter` font. Thus, later parts of the book consist of input and output dialogues where only the parts that appear after the equals sign are the input provided by the user. The following sections contain some examples.

1.1 Starting *Mathematica*

1.1.1 Text-oriented user interfaces

In these systems the program is started by inputting the command `math`. A message then appears, depending on the system and the version, followed by the input request `In[1]:=`. The user may now input a request, to which *Mathematica* will respond. This input has to be confirmed by striking the RETURN key. The following shows a screen display:

`In[1]:=`

If we input 2+5 the screen shows:

`In[1]:= 2+5`

When we press RETURN the screen shows:

`Out[1]= 7`

Note that only the calculation 2+5, not In[1] :=, must be keyed.
To leave *Mathematica* we simply input the Quit[ ] command.

To start *Mathematica*	math
To confirm input	RETURN
To leave *Mathematica*	Quit[]

Starting and closing Mathematica

1.1.2 Graphical user interfaces

In graphical user interface systems, like Windows on the PC, the program is activated by double-clicking on the *Mathematica* icon. The user is then presented with an empty workspace in which text and tasks can be entered in any sequence. In order to pass a section of material as a task for *Mathematica*, the input must be terminated by pressing SHIFT and RETURN at the same time.

Example – Input 2+5

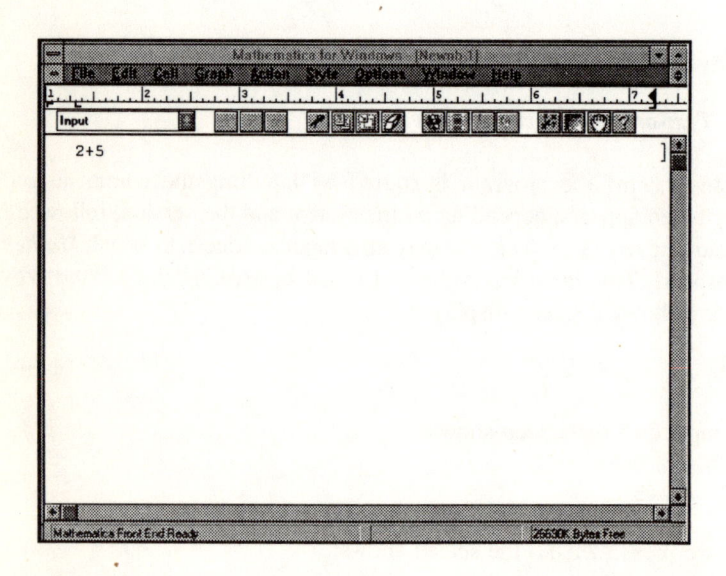

Press SHIFT and RETURN together

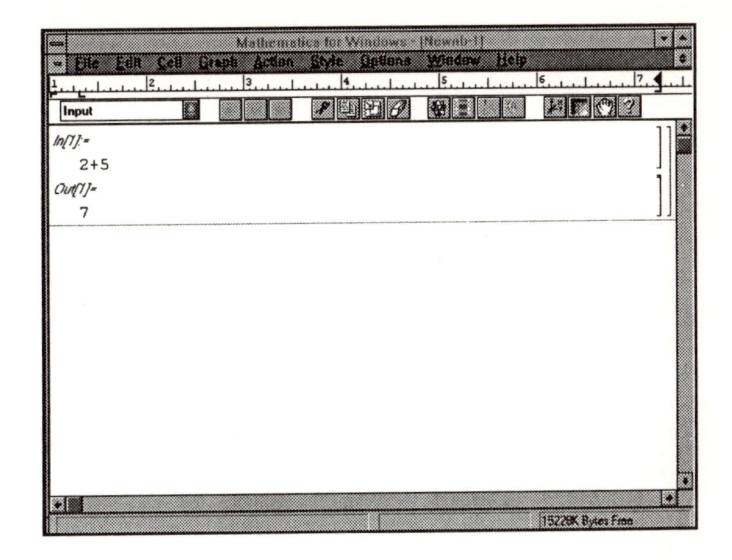

To start *Mathematica*	Double click *Mathematica* icon
To confirm input	Press SHIFT RETURN together
To leave *Mathematica*	Double click appropriate menu item

Starting and closing Mathematica

1.2 Calculating with numbers

Mathematica can be used very easily like a pocket calculator:

```
In[1]:=19-4
Out[1]=15
```

Of course, much larger numbers can be manipulated too:

```
In[2]:=1234567898767534*9876545676898765-3456432134567
Out[2]=12193266243410480070962354560943
```

In mathematics it is customary to leave a blank space instead of writing a multiplication sign. Such input is equally acceptable to *Mathematica*.

```
In[3]:=1234567898767534 9876545676898765-3456432134567
Out[3]=12193266243410480070962354560943
```

Of course, division is handled:

```
In[4]:=5/7
Out[4]=  5
         ─
         7
```

This output is unusual, for with a normal pocket calculator we would expect to get a decimal number. (Note that in this book a decimal number is understood to be a number that can be represented by the digits 0 to 9 and a decimal point.) Because *Mathematica* is a computer-based algebra system, which always calculates precisely, it uses the correct representation for all numbers — that is, there is no decimal rounding, unless specifically requested.

There is one way of making a decimal number from the numerator and denominator of the above fraction. This method of course also works if both are given in decimal form.

```
In[5]:=5./7
Out[5]=0.714286
```

In this case *Mathematica* assumes that a number was provided as a decimal and therefore provides the solution in decimal form.

The other way is to use the *Mathematica* function N[ ]. This function calculates a decimal approximation of the argument.

```
In[6]:=N[5/7]
Out[6]=0.714286
```

The total number of decimal places provided depends on the computer and the accuracy specified for the calculation. If more decimal places are required (say 20), this instruction can be given to the N function on every computer in the following way:

```
In[7]:=N[5/7, 20]
Out[7]=0.71428571428571428571
```

As can be seen from the input data, the number of places required is inserted, separated by a comma. *Mathematica* calculates with parentheses, in the usual way:

```
In[8]:=(7+9)/17
Out[8]=   16
          ──
          17
```

Again, the N function can be used to obtain a decimal approximation.

Introduction

We shall now introduce an example of raising to a power. The inventor of chess requested $2^{64} - 1$ grains of wheat as a reward from his king. *Mathematica* enables this figure to be calculated exactly.

```
In[9]:=2^64-1
Out[9]=18446744073709551615
```

With many pocket calculators it is also possible to calculate factorial functions; however, in the majority of cases this cannot be done for a number greater than 69. Here is an example for a somewhat larger number:

```
In[10]:=100!
Out[10]=9332621544394415268169923885626670049071596826\
        4381621468592963895217599993229915608941463976\
        5651828625369792082722375825118521091686400000\
        0000000000000000
```

The backslash (\) in the display is used as a separator to indicate that the data is continued in the subsequent lines.

The prime factors of 100! are quite easy to determine. FactorInteger is the *Mathematica* function to be used. The result of the previous calculation can be produced at the same time by appending the % symbol.

```
In[11]:=FactorInteger[%]
Out[11]={{2, 97}, {3, 48}, {5, 24}, {7, 16}, {11, 9},
        {13, 7}, {17, 5}, {19, 5}, {23, 4}, {29, 3},
        {31, 3}, {37, 2}, {41, 2}, {43, 2}, {47, 2},
        {53, 1}, {59, 1}, {61, 1}, {67, 1}, {71, 1},
        {73, 1}, {79, 1}, {83, 1}, {89, 1}, {97, 1}}
```

Here the output appears as a list, each element of which contains another list in which the first entry is the prime factor and the second is the frequency of the prime factor (see chapter 3 for more information). In addition, the structure of *Mathematica* commands is identifiable from the example.

- All *Mathematica* commands have an initial capital letter.
- If a command consists of more than one word, there is no space between words, and new words begin with a capital letter.
- The arguments of a command are placed within square brackets.

Structure of Mathematica commands

> - Addition, subtraction, multiplication and division are shown by the usual operator symbols (+ - * /).
> - The multiplication symbol (*) can be replaced by a blank space.
> - Raising to a power is shown by ^.
> - Factorials are shown by !.
> - To obtain a decimal approximation for a value, the function N[ ] is used. A specified number of decimal places can be obtained by adding the required number, separated by a comma.
> - The % symbol displays the last result.
> - The %% symbol displays the last but one result.
> - Inputting %n displays the result of the output line with Out[n].

Summary of calculation rules

1.3 Calculating with real numbers and functions

As already mentioned, *Mathematica* attempts to calculate exactly. For *Mathematica* this means that, for example, fractions are only shown in that form, and are not converted to decimal numbers. The effect that this has on calculation with roots, logarithms and function values of trigonometric functions is shown in this section.

First we give a few examples for calculating with roots. The *Mathematica* command for the square root is Sqrt[ ].

Exact calculation of $\sqrt{2} \sqrt{3}$:

```
In[1]:=Sqrt[2] Sqrt[3]
Out[1]=Sqrt[6]
```

Since $\sqrt{6}$ can neither be shown as a whole number nor as a fraction with whole number numerator and denominator, the result remains as it is.

```
In[2]:=Sqrt[144+25]
Out[2]=13
```

First the argument of the root function is calculated. Since it is a square, the root is also obtained. The next two examples illustrate the same process:

```
In[3]:=Sqrt[49/25-24/25]
Out[3]=1

In[4]:=Sqrt[173/64-23/16]
Out[4]=  9
         -
         8
```

Introduction

These examples show how *Mathematica* attempts to find the result by following the normal mathematical rules for calculating square roots. This is why the first example yielded the result Sqrt[6]. A decimal approximation is obtained if the number for which an approximation is required is indicated by a number with decimal point.

```
In[5]:=Sqrt[2.] Sqrt [3]
Out[5]=1.41421 Sqrt[3]
```

Because only the argument of the first root is indicated to be a decimal number, only this number is converted to a decimal. The second root remains as it is. The next example shows one way to obtain a decimal approximation for the result. Another way is to use the function N. (Both methods give the same result, assuming the same number of decimal places.)

```
In[6]:=Sqrt[2.] Sqrt[3]
Out[6]=2.44949
```

```
In[7]:=N[Sqrt[2] Sqrt[3],5]
Out[7]=2.44949
```

To calculate higher roots ($\sqrt[3]{x}$ ...), we must use the fractional exponent method of display ($\sqrt[n]{x} = x^{1/n}$). For logarithms, the commands Log[ ] for natural logarithms (with the Euler number *e* as base) and Log[Basis, x] for logarithms to any base are available. When inputting the command Log[Basis, x] the word Basis must be replaced by a number and *x* by a variable.

```
In[8]:=Log[E^3]
Out[8]=3
```

As can be seen, *Mathematica* uses E to represent the Euler number *e*.

```
In[9]:=Log[1000]
Out[9]=Log[1000]
```

Because 1000 is not a rational power of *e*, the exact result remains as ln 1000.

```
In[10]:=Log[1000.]
Out[10]=6.90776
```

Once again, the same procedures apply as we described for roots when expressions are represented. To calculate the logarithm of 1000 to base 10:

```
In[11]:=Log[10,1000]
Out[11]=3
```

```
In[12]:=Log[10,E]
Out[12]=       1
           --------
           Log[10]
```

This shows how *Mathematica* works internally with natural logarithms, as the result is shown by natural logarithms. The next example makes this clear:

```
In[13]:=Log[10,1024]
Out[13]=  Log[1024]
          ---------
          Log[10]

In[14]:=Log[2,1024]
Out[14]=10
```

For the exponential function to base *e*, *Mathematica* recognises the representations `E^x` and `Exp[x]`. Both can be used.

Root function ($\sqrt{x}$)	Sqrt[x]
Exponential function (e^x)	Exp[x] or E^x
Natural logarithmic function (ln x)	Log[x]
Logarithmic function to base b ($\log_b x$)	Log[b, x]

Functions in Mathematica

To calculate trigonometric functions, there are the following commands:

Sine function	Sin[x]
Cosine function	Cos[x]
Tangent function	Tan[x]
Cotangent function	Cot[x]
Secant function	Sec[x]
Cosecant function	Csc[x]

Trigonometric functions in Mathematica

On calling one of these functions *Mathematica* expects the argument to be supplied in the radian measure. Of course, inverse functions are available for all trigonometric functions. The names of these are obtained by putting `Arc` in front of the corresponding function name. Thus, `ArcCot[ ]` is the inverse function of `Cot[ ]`.

The number π is called by `Pi` in *Mathematica*. In the following examples the same representational procedures apply. *Mathematica* calculates the trigonometric functions for special values like $\pi/6$, $\pi/4$, $\pi/3$, etc., exactly, that is in the form of

Introduction

roots and fractions. If this is not possible, *Mathematica* does not change the input, but if necessary continues to calculate further with this exact result. If a decimal approximation is required for the value of the trigonometric function, this must be indicated by use of the decimal point or the N function.

```
In[15]:=Tan[pi/4]
Out[15]=1

In[16]:=Sin[5 Pi/6]
Out[16]= 1
         -
         2

In[17]:=Cos[Pi/6]
Out[17]= Sqrt[3]
         -------
            2

In[18]:=Cot[3]
Out[18]=Cot[3]

In[19]:=Cot[3.]
Out[19]=-7.01525

In[20]:=ArcSin[1/2]
Out[20]= Pi
         --
         6
```

Notice in these examples how the output is obtained. Because trigonometric functions of angles are often also required in degrees, *Mathematica* contains the constant Degree for transformation. Thus cos 45° is calculated by:

```
In[21]:=Cos[45 Degree]
Out[21]=Cos[45 Degree]
```

Unfortunately, on a PC at least, *Mathematica* does not simplify this value in the required form. However, a decimal approximation can be obtained:

```
In[22]:=N[Cos[45 Degree]]
Out[22]=0.707107
```

1.4 Calculating with complex numbers and functions

To represent complex numbers we need the imaginary unit i with $i^2 = -1$. *Mathematica* uses I for this. Complex numbers are input in the form a+ I b or a+ b I. We now give some examples for the basic types of calculation:

```
In[1]:=(3+ I 7) + (18- I 14)
Out[1]=21 - 7 I
```

```
In[2]:=(38+ I 27) * (17- I)
Out[2]=673 + 421 I
```

The multiplication symbol in the last example must not be included.

```
In[3]:=(16 + I 2)/(14+ I 3)
Out[3]= 46     4 I
        -- -  ---
        41    41

In[4]:=(16 + I Sqrt[2])/(14+ I Sqrt[3])
Out[4]=16 + I Sqrt[2]
       ---------------
       14 + I Sqrt[3]
```

Unfortunately, the last transformation is not quite what is required, because *Mathematica* only outputs the input term as a fraction and not simplified. It would be preferable if *Mathematica* were to transform the denominator into a real number by expanding with the complex conjugated denominator.

The following commands are available for the manipulation of complex numbers: Re[ ], Im[ ], Conjugate[ ], Abs[ ], Arg[ ]. Some examples show how they are used.

To calculate the real component:

```
In[5]:=Re[Pi+I 19]
Out[5]=Pi
```

To calculate the imaginary part:

```
In[6]:=Im[Pi + I 19]
Out[6]=19
```

To calculate the complex conjugate:

```
In[7]:=Conjugate[Pi + I 19]
Out[7]=-19 I + Pi
```

To calculate the modulus:

```
In[8]:=Abs[41 + I 19]
Out[8]=Sqrt[2042]
```

To calculate the argument with the Euler representation $e^{i\phi}$ of a complex number:

```
In[9]:=Arg[41 + I 19]
Out[9]=ArcTan[41, 19]

In[10]:=N[%]
Out[10]=0.433953
```

The following commands are available for the handling of complex numbers:

Representation	x + I y
Real part	Re[z]
Imaginary part	Im[z]
Modulus	Abs[z]
Argument	Arg[z]
Complex conjugate	Conjugate[z]

The functions described in the previous section can also be applied to complex arguments.

Complex functions

1.5 Problems

1. Find the prime factors of $2^{45} - 1$.
2. Calculate $\sqrt{17} \sqrt{68}$.
3. Calculate ln 335, together with a decimal approximation for the value.
4. Calculate $\log_4 2048$.
5. Calculate sin 135°, as well as a decimal approximation for the value.
6. Calculate the real part of the complex number $5 - 5i$.
7. Calculate the imaginary part of $5 - 5i$.
8. Calculate the sum of $5 - 5i$.
9. Calculate the argument of $5 - 5i$.

2 Term transformations

2.1 Calculating with symbols

The facilities of *Mathematica* outlined in the previous chapter are those of a very useful pocket calculator. The additional feature that distinguishes computer algebra systems like *Mathematica* is that they can calculate with symbols (variables, letters, etc.). Some indication of what calculating with symbols means was given in the previous chapter in the handling of function values. *Mathematica* calculated $\sqrt{2}\ \sqrt{3}$ as $\sqrt{6}$, and not 2.44949 as would be the case with a pocket calculator.

Using numbers we recall that:

```
In[1]:= 7+18-156.45+789/45
Out[1]= -113.917
```

Here the result is given as a decimal, because one number was input as a decimal and there are no further functions in the term.

Now, an example with symbols:

```
In[2]:= 4x -17a+14x-33a-9x
Out[2]= -50 a + 9 x
```

These examples show that *Mathematica* can operate with symbols as well as numbers. We shall see whether it also copes with the basic calculus for symbols:

```
In[3]:= (4x+17)*(3x-4)
Out[3]= (-4 + 3 x) (17 = 4 x)
```

This example shows that *Mathematica* returns the input in only slightly altered form, but does not carry out the desired calculation. To achieve this, further commands are required; these will be discussed in the following section. In order to evaluate terms that contain variables, one or more values are substituted for the variable. In *Mathematica* the equals sign (=) is used to assign a value.

```
In[4]:= x=7
Out[4]= 7
```

The above assigns the value 7 to the variable x. The following example shows the result of calculating the term $x^2 - 5$:

```
In[5]:= x^2-5
Out[5]= 44
```

The value shows that the value 7 is substituted for the variable *x*. Another example:

```
In[6]:= x^2-17x+3
Out[6]= -67
```

Because the last term is to be considered further, it is assigned to a variable with the name term. The descriptor term is written in lower-case letters, to avoid confusion with *Mathematica* commands (which always have an initial capital letter).

```
In[7]:= term=x^2-17x+3
Out[7]= -67
```

The term was correctly evaluated with the value 7 for variable *x*. We now give a further example with another value for *x*. First the value 5 is assigned to *x* and then the term is evaluated:

```
In[8]:= x=5
Out[8]= 5

In[9]:= term
Out[9]= -67
```

The result shows that when the assignment of the term variable occurs the term $x^2 - 17x + 3$ is not evaluated, but the value of this term for $x = 7$ is given. This is also illustrated by the following evaluation for $x = 5$.

```
In[10]:= x^2-17x+3
Out[10]= -57
```

Now, in order to ensure satisfactory output, all assignments have to be cancelled. This is done with command Clear[ ] or =..
  To clear the assignment for *x*:

```
In[11]:= Clear[x]
```

Using the alternative method to clear the assignment for the variable term:

```
In[12]:= term=.
```

The ? symbol can be used to find out the current assignment of a variable:

```
In[13]:= ?x
Out[13]= Global'x
```

```
In[14]:= ?term
Out[14]= Global'term
```

The outputs show that the variables are not reserved.

We now make another attempt to evaluate a term taking different values for the variables. In contrast to the earlier example we will begin with term and then take x:

```
In[15]:= term=x^2-17x+3
Out[15]=
                 2
         3 - 17 x + x

In[16]:= x=7
Out[16]= 7

In[17]:= term
Out[17]= -67

In[18]:= x=5
Out[18]= 5

In[19]:= term
Out[19]= -57
```

By this means the evaluation of the term for different values of x could be obtained. In the first procedure there occurs an early binding of the variables (before the assignment of the term); in the second there is late binding of the variables (after the assignment of the term). For this reason, before terms are assigned, one should check whether the variables contained in the term already have an assigned value.

Assignment of a value to a variable	x = value
Clearing of assignments	Clear[x] or x=.
Interrogation of assignments	?x

- Check thoroughly the values of variables contained in a term before evaluating it.
- Consider carefully which term to assign first and which term to assign later, especially when one depends on the other.

Assignment of variables

2.2 Calculating with rational integral terms

As mentioned in the previous section, *Mathematica* commands are used to multiply out an expression within brackets. One of these commands is

Term transformations

Expand[ ]. Here is a first example:

```
In[1]:= Expand[(x-17)(x+a)]
Out[1]=
         -17 a - 17 x + a x + x^2
```

Now, two more extensive examples:

```
In[2]:= Expand[(x-Pi)^15]
Out[2]=
    -Pi^15 + 15 Pi^14 x - 105 Pi^13 x^2 + 455 Pi^12 x^3 -
    1365 Pi^11 x^4 + 3003 Pi^10 x^5 - 5005 Pi^9 x^6 +
    6435 Pi^8 x^7 - 6435 Pi^7 x^8 + 5005 Pi^6 x^9 -
    3003 Pi^5 x^10 + 1365 Pi^4 x^11 - 455 Pi^3 x^12 +
    105 Pi^2 x^13 - 15 Pi x^14 + x^15

In[3]:= Expand[(x-a+5)^7]
Out[3]=
    78125 - 109375 a + 65625 a^2 - 21875 a^3 + 4375 a^4 -
    525 a^5 + 35 a^6 - a^7 + 109375 x - 131250 a x +
    65625 a^2 x - 17500 a^3 x + 2625 a^4 x - 210 a^5 x +
    7 a^6 x + 65625 x^2 - 65625 a x^2 + 26250 a^2 x^2 -
    5250 a^3 x^2 + 525 a^4 x^2 - 21 a^5 x^2 + 21875 x^3 -
    17500 a x^3 + 5250 a^2 x^3 - 700 a^3 x^3 + 35 a^4 x^3 +
    4375 x^4 - 2625 a x^4 + 525 a^2 x^4 - 35 a^3 x^4 +
    525 x^5 - 210 a x^5 + 21 a^2 x^5 + 35 x^6 - 7 a x^6 + x^7
```

The calculations for these examples are carried out very fast; however, because of its length, the output is somewhat obscure.

For many calculations often only the first and/or last terms are needed. In such cases the command Short can be used. Here is an illustration using the last example:

```
In[4]:= Short[%]
Out[4]//Short=
                78125 - 109375 a + <<33>> + x^7
```

The last example was called by the % and Short was applied to it. The output contains the first two terms and the last; the total of those not displayed is shown within double angle brackets. If more lines of the term are required, the number of display lines can be appended as a second command to the Short command:

```
In[5]:= Short[%%,2]
Out[5]//Short=
                      2             3
78125 - 109375 a + 65625 a  - 21875 a  + <<30>> -
      6    7
   7 a x  + x
```

This gives a two-line output. If we want to have the output of an expanded expression in short form immediately, there are two possibilities. One way is to pass the result of the Expand command as argument to the Short command:

```
In[6]:= Short[Expand[(x+1)^105],2]
Out[6]//Short=
                 2           3
1 + 105 x + 5460 x  + 187460 x  + <<100>> +
         104    105
   105 x    + x
```

By the other means the output from the expansion is suppressed by ending the command with a semicolon and then following with the Short command:

```
In[7]:= Expand[x+1)^105];

In[7]:= Short[%]
Out[8]//Short=                      105
          1 + 105 x + <<103>> + x
```

Most frequently required are parts of an expanded term. *Mathematica* contains three functions for this. To illustrate how they work a term (t) is used:

```
In[9]:= t=Expand[x-y+41]^4-(x+y-17)^2]
Out[9]=
                          2         3     4
2825472 + 275718 x + 10085 x  + 164 x  + x  -
                           2          3
275650 y - 20174 x y - 492 x y - 4 x  y +
       2        2       2          3       3       4
  10085 y + 492 x y  + 6 x  y  - 164 y - 4 x y  + y
```

For example, the coefficients of *x* in *t* can be obtained with the Coefficient command:

```
In[10]:= Coefficient[t,x]
Out[10]=                       2       3
           275718 - 20174 y + 492 y  - 4 y
```

This produces all coefficients, including those that contain powers of *y*. The highest exponents, say, of *y* in *t*, can be obtained with the Exponent command:

```
In[11]:= Exponent[t,y]
Out[11]= 4
```

The expanded term shows that the highest exponent of *y* is 4. In order, say, to

Term transformations

obtain the seventh term in *t*, the Part command is used:

```
In[12]:= Part[t,7]
Out[12]= -20174 x y
```

Hitherto, we have shown the detailed multiplying out and summarising of rational integral terms. However, one often needs the problem to be presented the other way round, if the factors of a term are required. The command Factor sees to this. To obtain the factors of the term $x^3 - 6x^2 + 11x - 6$:

```
In[13]:= Factor[x^3-6x^2+11x-6]
Out[13]= (-3 + x) (-2 + x) (-1 + x)

In[14]:= Factor[100 x^3-135x^2+100x-135]
                            2
Out[14]= 5 (-27 + 20 x) (1 + x)
```

The representation contains only real factors. To obtain all of them, including the complex ones, the option of the command Factor must be altered. This option is called GaussianInteger and its default setting is False; this must be changed to True when complex factors are to be obtained. An arrow -> points to the assignment of a new value:

```
In[15]:= Factor[100 x^3-135x^2+100x-135,
                GaussianIntegers->True]
Out[15]= 5 (-I + x) (I + x) (-27 + 20 x)
```

Expand (multiply out, summarise) a term	Expand[*exp*]
Short representation of a term	Short[*exp*]
Short representation of a term in n lines	Short[*exp*, *n*]
Factorise a term with real factors	Factor[*exp*]
Factorise a term with complex factors	Factor[*exp*, GaussianIntegers->True]
Coefficients of a variable	Coefficient[*exp*, *var*]
Largest exponent of a variable	Exponent[*exp*, *var*]
Determination of the nth term in an expression	Part[*exp*, *n*]
Suppression of the task	Append a semicolon (;) to the command

Commands for rational integral terms

2.3 Calculating with fractions (rational expressions)

The commands described in the previous section can also be used on fractions. Before we look at these, we shall first introduce the `Simplify` command, which can be used to summarise and simplify both terms and fractions:

```
In[1]:= Simplify[(x^3-1)/(x-1)]
                  2
Out[1]=   1 + x + x
```

The following example shows that the command `Simplify` both reduces and summarises fractions:

```
In[2]:= Simplify[((x^6+a^6)(x+1))/
                 ((x^6+a^6)(x^2-a^2)+a^2x^2(x^4-a^4))+/
                 (a^2 x^2(x+1))/(x^6-a^6-a^2 x^2(x^2 -a^2))]
Out[2]=   1 + x
          --------
            2     2
          -a  + x
```

To illustrate the effect of some *Mathematica* commands on fractions, we will establish a variable with the name `fraction`.

```
In[3]:= fraction=((x-3)(x+5)^2 (x-7))/((x+1)(x-2)^2)
Out[3]=                           2
          (-7 + x) (-3 + x) (5 + x)
          ---------------------------
                   2
          (-2 + x)  (1 + x)
```

To multiply out the numbers of this fraction, the `Expand` command is used:

```
In[4]:= Expand[fraction]
Out[4]=       525                  40 x
         ----------------  -  ----------------  -
                2                     2
         (-2 + x) (1 + x)      (-2 + x) (1 + x)
                                         4
              54 x                     x
         ----------------  +  ----------------
                2                     2
         (-2 + x) (1 + x)      (-2 + x) (1 + x)
```

As can be seen, only the numerator is multiplied out, while the denominator remains in factorised form. Furthermore, we can see that the result is shown as the sum of single fractions, in which all the denominators are the same and the powers increase in the numerator. If both numerator and denominator are to be multiplied out in a fraction, the `ExpandAll` command must be used:

Term transformations

```
In[5]:= ExpandAll[fraction]
```
$$\text{Out[5]}= \frac{525}{4 - 3x^2 + x^3} - \frac{40x}{4 - 3x^2 + x^3} - \frac{54x^2}{4 - 3x^2 + x^3} + \frac{x^4}{4 - 3x^2 + x^3}$$

To produce the result not as the sum of single fractions, the Together command is used. (Remember that the previous output can be recalled with the % symbol.)

```
In[6]:= Together[%]
```
$$\text{Out[6]}= \frac{525 - 40x - 54x^2 + x^4}{4 - 3x^2 + x^3}$$

To produce a sum of single fractions from such a compact fraction as the previous output, the Apart command is used:

```
In[7]:= Apart[%]
```
$$\text{Out[7]}= 3 + \frac{245}{3(-2 + x)} - \frac{917}{9(-2 + x)} + x + \frac{512}{9(1 + x)}$$

As can be seen, not only are partial fractions produced – as were produced for the example above by the Expand command – but the partial fractions are reduced as much as possible. If the Factor command is invoked, the total is summarised and the result factorised into numerator and denominator. Thus in this example the output term that was input for the fraction is obtained:

```
In[8]:= Factor[%]
```
$$\text{Out[8]}= \frac{(-7 + x)(-3 + x)(5 + x)^2}{(-2 + x)^2(1 + x)}$$

To be able to recall the numerator and denominator of a fraction, the Numerator and Denominator commands are available:

```
In[9]:= Numerator[fraction]
```
$$\text{Out[9]}= (-7 + x)(-3 + x)(5 + x)^2$$

```
In[10]:= Denominator[fraction]
```
$$\text{Out[10]}= (-2 + x)^2(1 + x)$$

To simplify terms	`Simplify[exp]`
To multiply out the numerator of a fraction	`Expand[exp]`
To multiply out the numerator and denominator of a fraction	`ExpandAll[exp]`
To summarise fractions	`Together[exp]`
To separate fractions into partial fractions	`Apart[exp]`
To factorise the numerator and denominator of a fraction	`Factor[exp]`
Numerator of a fraction	`Numerator[exp]`
Denominator of a fraction	`Denominator[exp]`

Calculating with fractions

2.4 Problems

1. Calculate $(x + y - 17)(x^2 + 14x - 37)$.
2. Determine the coefficients of y in the term $(x + y - 17)(x^2 + 14x - 37)$.
3. Determine the highest power of x in the term $(x + y - 17)(x^2 + 14x - 37)$.
4. Calculate all linear functions of the term $3x^5 - 5x^4 - 27x^3 + 45x^2 - 1200x + 2000$.
5. Calculate

$$\frac{x^2 - 5x + 6}{x - 3}$$

6. Multiply out the numerator of the expression

$$\frac{(x - 5)(x + 14)}{(x + 11)(x - 17)}$$

7. Multiply out the numerator and denominator of the expression

$$\frac{(x - 5)(x + 14)}{(x + 11)(x - 17)}$$

8. Summarise the result of problem 7 into a rational expression.
9. Write the following in simplest partial fractions:

$$\frac{(x - 5)(x + 14)}{(x + 11)(x - 17)}$$

3 Lists, tables and functions

3.1 Lists

For many mathematical packages, including *Mathematica*, lists are elementary data types, that enable vectors, matrices and tensors to be represented. This section will discuss elementary operations with lists. A later chapter will examine calculating with vectors and matrices.

In *Mathematica* a list is understood to be a summary of objects. The objects that are to be summarised are identified by separating them by commas and enclosing them in curly brackets. The following examples show those objects that can be summarised in a list:

```
In[1]:= l1={a,b,c}
Out[1]= {a, b, c}

In[2]:= l2={1,2,3}
Out[2]= {1, 2, 3}

In[3]:= l3={l1,l1,l2}
Out[3]= {{a, b, c}, {a, b, c}, {1, 2, 3}}
```

Viewed mathematically, the first two examples can be interpreted as points or vectors, while the third is a matrix. However, this interpretation is not compulsory, since *Mathematica* can just as well calculate with these lists as with numbers:

```
In[4]:= l1 + l2
Out[4]= {1 + a, 2 + b, 3 + c}

In[5]:= l1 * l2
Out[5]= {a, 2 b, 3 c}

In[6]:= l1 / l2
Out[6]=       b   c
        {a,  -,  -}
              2   3

In[7]:= l1 ^ l2
Out[7]=        2    3
        {a,  b ,  c }
```

As these examples demonstrate, *Mathematica*'s procedures for calculating multiplication, division and raising to a power do not follow the normal rules of vector calculus. However, they are well adapted to producing tables, for example, as can be seen from examples 4 to 7.

To select one element in a list, the command Part or its alternative [[ ]] is used. So the second element from the first list is obtained by

```
In[8]:= Part[l1,2]
Out[8]= b
```

or by

```
In[9]:= l1[[2]]
Out[9]= b
```

With the third list the situation is more complicated, For example, to obtain the first element from the third entry, the following input can be tried:

```
In[10]:= Part[l3,{3,1}]
Out[10]= {{1, 2, 3}, {a, b, c}}
```

Unfortunately, this is not the required result, but a list that contains the third and the first entry of list l3. To obtain the required element we input

```
In[11]:= Part[l3,3,1]
Out[11]= 1
```

From the last two examples we establish:

- If we want to summarise parts of a list into a list of parts, we indicate to the Part command the locations of the corresponding parts in the list, separating them by commas, and enclosing them between curly brackets (see examples). The result is then always a list.

- If we want to select list elements of a list over different planes, after identifying the relevant list we indicate to the Part command those locations that we wish to consider in the single plane (see examples).

To change elements in a list, the Part command is used to call the element to be changed and the equals sign assigns a new value to it.

```
In[12]:= Part[l3,2,3]=x
Out[12]= x
```

The change can be seen when the list is examined:

```
In[13]:= l3
Out[13]= {{a, b, c}, {a, b, x}, {1, 2, 3}}
```

Lists, tables and functions 23

The elements of a list are summarised within curly brackets.	
To obtain an element in the list	Part[*list*, *i*]
	or list [[*i*]]
To obtain several elements in the list	Part[*list*,{*i*, *j*,...}]
	or list [[{*i*, *j*...}]]
To obtain elements from several planes in a list	Part[*list*, *i*, *j*,...]
	or list [[*i*, *j*...]]

Basic commands for lists

3.2 Tables

To produce a table, we can enter all the elements of the table by hand into a list. As this method is somewhat tedious, *Mathematica* contains the Table command. The following examples illustrate the application of this command. The third power of the natural numbers from 1 to 10 is obtained by:

```
In[1]:= Table[i^3,{i,1,10}]
Out[1]= {1, 8, 27, 64, 125, 216, 343, 512, 729, 1000}
```

In the input we see that the term(s) to be tabulated is passed as first argument to the Table command, while as second argument the domain for the current variable – in this example *i* – is specified. The table of the previous example becomes more readable if we output the associated current variable with every third power:

```
In[2]:= Table [{i,i^3},{i,1,10}]
Out[2]= {{1, 1}, {2, 8}, {3, 27}, {4, 64}, {5, 125},/
        {6, 216}, {7, 343}, {8, 512}, {9, 729}, {10, 1000}}
```

This output is already more readable than the last, but the display still does not conform to the usual style for tables. This is achieved by using the command TableForm:

```
In[3]:= TableForm[%]
Out[3]//TableForm=
1    1
2    8
3    27
4    64
5    125
6    216
7    343
8    512
9    729
10   1000
```

Using the sine function, the following example shows how the `Table` command can produce a table of values of a function:

```
In[4]:= Table[{x,Sin[x]},{x,0,Pi,Pi/6}]
Out[4]=        Pi   1       Pi   Sqrt[3]
        {{0, 0}, {--, -}, {--, -------},
                 6   2      3      2

         Pi         2 Pi   Sqrt[3]      5 Pi    1
        {--, 1}, {----, -------}, {----. -},
         2          3       2           6      2

         {Pi, 0}}
```

In the input we see that the step for the raising (lowering, in the case of negative values) of the variables can be specified in the setting of the table domain as the fourth parameter. If this parameter is not given, its default value is 1. In the following example the numerical approximations of the previous table are given in tabular form:

```
In[5]:= TableForm[N[%]]
Out[5]//TableForm=
0              0
0.523599       0.5
1.0472         0.866025
1.5708         1.
2.0944         0.866025
2.61799        0.5
3.14159        0
```

To produce a table	`Table[exp, {x, xmin, xmax, dx}]`
To produce a table with several variables	`Table[exp, {x, xmin, xmax, dx}, {y, ymin, ymax, dy},...]`
To form a table	`TableForm[list]`

exp   :term or a list of terms
x   :variable that will be altered
xmin :smallest value of x
xmax :greatest value of x
dx   :step for x

If dx is not given, the variable is increased by 1.

Commands to produce tables

3.3 Functions

In *Mathematica*, functions are defined in the same way as in mathematics – that is, a function can have one or several arguments, and the calculation of the function value is carried out with the aid of a functional equation. The variables of a function are described by defining with an underscore _. If several are involved, they are separated by commas. All arguments are enclosed within square brackets. Assignment of the function term is by :=. Here are some examples:

```
In[1]:= f[x_]:=x^3-x
```

To determine the function value at a location, say 1, the function is called by its associated argument:

```
In[2]:= f[1]
Out[2]= 0
```

Now, an example for a function with two variables:

```
In[3]:= g[x_,y_]:=x^2-y^2
```

The function value at a location is found as above:

```
In[4]:= g[1,2]
Out[4]= -3
```

We see that for *x* the value 1 and for *y* the value 2 is entered. g[x,y] is calculated with these values. But what happens if the function g is called with only one argument?

```
In[5]:= g[7]
Out[5]= g[7]
```

The output shows that *Mathematica* knows no rule for the calculation of g[7]. So the value is unchanged. If we now add to the above definition of f a further definition, then we can now call f with one or with two arguments:

```
In[6]:= f[x_,y_]:= x * Sin[y]

In[7]:= f[2,3]
Out[7]= 2 Sin[3]

In[8]:= f[2]
Out[8]= 6
```

Mathematica now knows one rule for the evaluation of f with one argument and another with two arguments. The method described here is fascinating, but should be used with care – that is, with precise planning.

In *Mathematica*, functions can be used not only to realise mathematical functions, but also to program. A later section describes this programming technique (see Chapter 8).

When defining functions, do not forget to include the underscore when inputting variables, otherwise some unexpected results will be obtained:

```
In[9]:= h[x]:=x^2+4

In[10]:= h[3]
Out[10]= h[3]

In[11]:= h[x]
Out[11]=      2
         4 + x
```

From the output we see that there is no rule available for the calculation of h[3] because *Mathematica* takes the x without underscore to be a fixed symbol, instead of a variable.

Assignment of the function term	=:
Variable descriptor	var_

Functions

3.4 Problems

1. Define the function f with $f(x) = x \cdot \sin x$ in *Mathematica*.
2. Produce a table of values of function f from problem 1 as x ranges in value from 0 to 2π in steps of $\pi/6$.
3. Find with *Mathematica* the fifth displayed point of the table from problem 2.
4. Find with *Mathematica* the value of the function at $\pi/2$ in the table from problem 2.

4 Solution of equations

Solving equations is an important task for algebra. Part of such tasks can be undertaken by software packages like *Mathematica*. Those tasks that can, and cannot, be handled by *Mathematica* are described in the next section.

4.1 Solution of rational integral equations

The category of rational integral equations is generally understood to include polynomials with integer coefficients, i.e. terms of the form

$$a_n x^n + a_{n-1} x^{n-1} + \ldots + a_0,$$

which do not contain root terms, trigonometric functions, etc. By means of the following examples we shall show how *Mathematica* can be used to solve equations.

First, we shall determine the solution of $3x + 7 = 14$. For this *Mathematica* has the Solve command:

```
In[1]:= Solve[3x+7==14,x]
Out[1]=         7
         {{x -> -}}
                3
```

This example shows how a double equals sign must be written with equations in *Mathematica*. The simple single equals sign cannot be used because it is already used in *Mathematica* for the assignment of values. In addition to the equation itself, a solution variable must be added to the Solve command, separated from the equation by a comma. The following example demonstrates why:

```
In[2]:= Solve[a x + b == 17,x]
Out[2]=              -17 + b
         {{x -> -(-------)}}
                      a
```

Here the equation is solved for x.

```
In[3]:= Solve[a x + b == 17,a]
Out[3]=              -17 + b
         {{a -> -(-------)}}
                      x
```

27

Here the equation is solved for *a*.

```
In[4]:= Solve[a x + b == 17,b]
Out[4]= {{b -> 17 - a x}}
```

Here the equation is solved for *b*.

In the equation $ax + b = 17$ it is not clear from the presentation for which of the three variables the equation is to be solved. Therefore, whoever is to solve the problem (in this case *Mathematica*), must be informed for which variable the equation is to be solved. Also, because the aim in *Mathematica* is to maintain a consistent syntax for the commands, it is necessary always to provide the solution variable, even when there is only one.

The next two examples show how *Mathematica* can be used to solve quadratic equations:

```
In[5]:= Solve[-x^2+x+6==0,x]
Out[5]= {{x -> -2}, {x -> 3}}

In[6]:= Solve[12x^2+2x==9x^2+9x-2,x]
Out[6]=         1
        {{x -> -}, {x -> 2}}
              3
```

From the last example we see how the equation does not necessarily have to be input in the form term [x] = 0. *Mathematica* can also solve quadratic equations with parameters:

```
In[7]:= Solve[3 a^2 x^2 + 4 a x +1==0,x]
Out[7]=         1              -1
        {{x -> -(-)}, {x -> ---}}
                a             3 a
```

With such equations, the question now arises as to whether it is solvable for every choice of parameter. To investigate this question the Reduce command can be invoked:

```
In[8]:= Reduce[3 a^2 x^2 + 4 a x +1==0,x]
Out[8]=              1            -1
        a != 0 && (x == -(-) || x == ---)
                         a            3 a
```

As can be seen, the syntax for Reduce is identical with that of Solve. Only the display of the solution differs. Before we examine this, we first explain the unknown symbols in the output. The != corresponds to the ≠ symbol, the && to the logical AND (∧) and the || to the logical OR (∨). If we now consider the output, we see that there is only a solution for $a \neq 0$.

Here now is a more complex quadratic equation:

Solution of equations

```
In[9]:= Reduce[3 a^2 x^2 + 4 a x +b==0,x]
Out[9]=   a != 0 && (x ==
```

$$x == \frac{-\frac{4}{a} + \frac{2\,\text{Sqrt}[4 - 3\,b]}{a}}{6} \;\;||$$

$$x == \frac{-\frac{4}{a} - \frac{2\,\text{Sqrt}[4 - 3\,b]}{a}}{6}) \;\;||$$

a == 0 && b == 0

Mathematica can also solve cubic equations:

```
In[10]:= Solve[x^3+x^2-4x-4==0,x]
Out[10]=  {{x -> -1}, {x -> -2}, {x -> 2}}
```

Now an example with somewhat different coefficients:

```
In[11]:= Solve[11 x^3-20 x^2- 10 x +22==0,x]
Out[11]=
```

$$\{\{x \to \frac{20}{33} + \frac{730\,(-1)^{11/6}}{33\,(18037\,I + 11\,\text{Sqrt}[526311])^{1/3}} +$$

$$\frac{(-1)^{1/6}\,(18037\,I + 11\,\text{Sqrt}[526311])^{1/3}}{33}\},$$

$$\{x \to \frac{20}{33} + \frac{I}{2}\,\text{Sqrt}[3]$$

$$(\frac{730\,(-1)^{5/6}}{33\,(18037\,I + 11\,\text{Sqrt}[526311])^{1/3}} +$$

$$\frac{(-1)^{1/6}\,(18037\,I + 11\,\text{Sqrt}[526311])^{1/3}}{33}) -$$

$$(\frac{730\,(-1)^{11/6}}{33\,(18037\,I + 11\,\text{Sqrt}[526311])^{1/3}} +$$

$$\frac{(-1)^{1/6}\,(18037\,I + 11\,\text{Sqrt}[526311])^{1/3}}{33}) / 2\},$$

```
             20   I
     {x ->  ---- - - Sqrt[3]
             33   2
                                5/6
                      730 (-1)
         (----------------------------- +
                                         1/3
            33 (18037 I + 11 Sqrt[526311])

                 1/6                          1/3
            (-1)    (18037 I + 11 Sqrt[526311])
            --------------------------------------) -
                              33

                                11/6
                      730 (-1)
         (----------------------------- +
                                         1/3
            33 (18037 I + 11 Sqrt[526311])

                 1/6                          1/3
            (-1)    (18037 I + 11 Sqrt[526311])
            --------------------------------------) / 2}}
                              33
```

As this output is rather involved, a numerical approximation can be obtained using N:

```
In[12]:= N[%]
Out[12]=
                                      -16
              {{x -> 1.61319 - 2.22045 10    I},

                                       -16
               {x -> -1.01567 + 3.03319 10    I},

                                      -17
               {x -> 1.22065 - 8.1274 10    I}}
```

Unfortunately, these values are false, because they all contain an imaginary part, albeit very small, even though all solutions are real. The reason for this error is to be found in *Mathematica*'s internal calculating precision. For some time similar problems have been described in discussions about *Mathematica*. It is not known for what reason the producer has not yet eliminated this error.

In order to obtain the correct numerical solutions for this example, we must use the NSolve command. Then the above-mentioned problems do not occur. The syntax of this command accords with that of the Solve command:

```
In[13]:= NSolve[11 x^3-20 x^2- 10 x +22==0,x]
Out[13]=   {{x -> -1.0156658802924896},
            {x -> 1.220654426396538},
            {x -> 1.61319327207777}}
```

Mathematica allows higher-order equations to be solved as well. In general, from the theory of equations, this is only possible symbolically for equations of degree 4 at the most. *Mathematica* indeed attempts to solve equations symbolically that are of an even higher degree, but then runs up against its limits.

Solution of equations

Here are some examples:

```
In[14]:= Expand[(x^2+2)(x^2-4)(x^2+7)]
Out[14]=         2     4    6
         -56 - 22 x + 5 x + x
```

```
In[15]:= Solve[%==0,x]
Out[15]= {{x -> I Sqrt[2]}, {x -> -I Sqrt[2]},
 {x -> I Sqrt[7]}, {x -> -I Sqrt[7]}, {x -> 2},
 {x -> -2}}
```

```
In[16]:= Solve{x^8-17 x^7+19 x^6+43 x^3-37x^2+41==0,x]
Out[16}=                    2       3       6       7
          {ToRules[Roots[-37 x + 43 x + 19 x - 17 x
                  8
                + x  == -41, x]]}
```

The output ToRules means that *Mathematica* cannot carry out any further reduction of the solutions (Roots). Therefore the symbolic (in this case the original) expression survives. The Roots command is used in order to solve one (!) equation. Because the Solve command can be applied more generally, it has been used up until now and will also be employed more widely.

The numerical solutions of the previous example can be found with NSolve.

```
In[17]:= NSolve[x^8-17 x^7+19 x^6+43 x^3-37x^2+41==0,x]
Out[17]= {{x -> -1.03511}, {x -> -0.863439},
         {x -> -0.0475751 - 1.31185 I},
         {x _> -0.0475751 + 1.31185 I},
         {x -> 0.768138 - 0.651644 I},
         {x -> 0.768138 + 0.651644 I}, {x -> 1.66087},
         {x -> 15.7966}}
```

4.2 Equations with square roots and absolute values

Apart from purely algebraic equations, *Mathematica* can also solve those that can be reduced to the algebraic. Roots and sum equations are two representatives of this category.

```
In[1]:= Solve[Sqrt[x+4]==4,x]
Out[1]= {{x -> 12}}
```

```
In[2]:= Solve[x+Sqrt[x]==3,x]
Out[2]=         7 + Sqrt[13]        7 - Sqrt[13]
        {{x -> -------------}, {x -> -------------}}
                    2                     2
```

In order to obtain the correct solutions with root equations, a test must be carried out with all solutions.

In the first example the evaluating of the right and left side of the equation for $x = 12$ gives the value 4. In the second example the test is rather more difficult to carry out, so it should be undertaken by *Mathematica*. Because the right side of the equation is still 3, only the left side is evaluated for the differential solutions using the ls (left side) function defined below:

```
In[3]:= ls[x_]:= x+Sqrt[x]
```

First, the test for the left side:

```
In[4]:= ls[(7+Sqrt[13])/2]
Out[4]=   Sqrt[7 + Sqrt[13]]     7 + Sqrt[13]
        ------------------  +   ------------
              Sqrt[2]                 2
```

Now, the attempt to reduce the expression with the Simplify command:

```
In[5]:= Simplify[(Sqrt{7+Sqrt[13]])/Sqrt[2]+
                 (7+Sqrt[13])/2]
Out[5]=   (7 + Sqrt[13] +
          Sqrt[2] Sqrt[7 + Sqrt[13]]) / 2
```

The following numerical approximation shows that the first solution is not a solution to the root equation:

```
In[6]:= N[%]
Out[6]=   7.60555
```

Now the test for the second solution with reduction and numerical approximation:

```
In[7]:= ls[7-Sqrt[13])/2]
Out[7]=   Sqrt[7 - Sqrt[13]]     7 - Sqrt[13]
        ------------------  +   ------------
              Sqrt[2]                 2

In[8]:= Simplify[(Sqrt[7-Sqrt[13]])/Sqrt[2]+
                 (7-Sqrt[13])/2]
Out[8]=   (7 - Sqrt[13] +
          Sqrt[2] Sqrt[7 - Sqrt[13]]) / 2

In[9]:= N[%]
Out[9]=   3.
```

At least, the numerical approximation shows that the second solution is also a solution to the root equation. Because the procedure described here for carrying out the test is extravagant, *Mathematica* contains an option for the Solve command which carries out the test automatically. This option is VerifySolutions, which has the default value False. The following input illustrates how the option is used:

```
In[10]:= Solve[x+Sqrt[x]==3,x,VerifySolutions->True]
Out[10]=             7 - Sqrt[13]
             {{x ->  ------------}}
                          2
```

We shall now consider an example involving the absolute value function:

```
In[11]:= Solve[Abs[x^2-10x+20]==4,x]
Out[11]=
                              (-1)
            10 + 2 Sqrt[5 + Abs    [4]]
      {{x -> ------------------------------},
                         2

                              (-1)
            10 - 2 Sqrt[5 + Abs    [4]]
       {x -> ------------------------------}}
                         2

In[12]:= Solve[Abs[x^2-10x+20]==4,x,
              VerifySolutions->True]
Out[12]=
                              (-1)
            10 + 2 Sqrt[5 + Abs    [4]]
      {{x -> ------------------------------},
                         2

                              (-1)
            10 - 2 Sqrt[5 + Abs    [4]]
       {x -> ------------------------------}}
                         2
```

However the `VerifySolutions` options is set, the solution is shown by means of the inverse function of the absolute value function. Unfortunately, the solution does not provide much. By using N, approximate values can be determined, as this equation is solvable algebraically; but another way is shown here which manages without the inverse function of the absolute value. In mathematics, the identity $|x| = \sqrt{x^2}$ is shown for real numbers of x. If on the basis of this identity the absolute value is substituted, correct solutions are obtained. The `VerifySolutions` option, for safety's sake set at `True`, because of the root, should be used.

```
In[13]:= Solve[Sqrt[(x^2-10x+20)^2]==4,x,
              VerifySolutions->True]
Out[13]=  {{x -> 8}, {x -> 2}, {x -> 6},
           {x -> 4}}
```

This yields all solutions.

4.3 Trigonometric equations

With trigonometric equations, problems similar to those found above often occur. Here is a simple example:

```
In[1]:= Solve[Sin[x]==Cos[x],x]
Out[1]=
Solve::ifun:
    Warning: Inverse functions are being
       used by Solve, so some solutions
       may not be found.
```

```
Solve::tdep:
   The equations appear to involve
      transcendental functions of the
      variables in an essentially
      non-algebraic way.

Solve[Sin[x] == Cos[x],x]
```

In the output the equation remains unchanged and error messages appear, which draw attention to the problematic use of trigonometric inverse functions and their inverse functions in equations. A frequently used method of solving trigonometric equations is to transform them into algebraic equations with the aid of the trigonometric Pythagorean theorem ($\sin^2 x + \cos^2 x = 1$). This additional information can be passed to the Solve command as a further equation. Because two equations are passed to the Solve command, these must be enclosed in curly brackets:

```
In[2]:- Solve[{Sin[x]==Cos[x],Sin[x]^2+Cos[x]^2==1},x]
Out[2]=
Solve::ifun:
   Warning: Inverse functions are being
      used by Solve, so some solutions
      may not be found.

Solve::tdep:
   The equations appear to involve
      transcendental functions of the
      variables in an essentially
      non-algebraic way.

Solve[{Sin[x] == Cos[x],
            2           2
      Cos[x]  + Sin[x]   == 1}, x]
```

But even this additional equation does not yield the required result, because it is not an algebraic equation in x, but in Sin[x]. So the Sin[x] equation must first be solved:

```
In[3]:= Solve[{Sin[x]==Cos[x],Sin[x]^2+Cos[x]^2==1},
            Sin[x]]
Out[3]=  {}
```

This is, however, still not the required solution. Because in both equations the sine and cosine terms have equal status, the equation should also be solved for both:

```
In[4]:= Solve[{Sin[x]==Cos[x],Sin[x]^2+Cos[x]^2==1},
            {Sin[x],Cos[x]}]
Out[4]=                  1
            {{Sin[x] -> -------,
                        Sqrt[2]
```

Solution of equations

$$\text{Cos}[x] \to \frac{1}{\text{Sqrt}[2]}\},$$

$$\{\text{Sin}[x] \to -(\frac{1}{\text{Sqrt}[2]}),$$

$$\text{Cos}[x] \to -(\frac{1}{\text{Sqrt}[2]})\}\}$$

As can be seen, this method is successful. To determine the *x* values, the four equations must then be solved for *x*:

```
In[5]:= Solve[Sin[x]==1/Sqrt[2],x]
Out[5]=
Solve::ifun:
   Warning: Inverse functions are being
     used by Solve, so some solutions
     may not be found.
```

$$\{\{x \to \text{ArcSin}[\frac{1}{\text{Sqrt}[2]}]\}\}$$

Unfortunately, the solutions to the other equations yield similar unattractive outputs. This is most regrettable, because these equations have exact solutions of $\pi/2$ or $-\pi/2$. Chapter 8 describes how this can be rectified. The following examples examine whether the above-mentioned method can be applied with other trigonometric equations:

```
In[6]:= Solve[{Cos[x]+ 4 Sin[x]==0,Sin[x]^2+
           Cos[x]^2==1}, {Sin[x],Cos[x]}]
Out[6]=
```
$$\{\{\text{Sin}[x] \to -(\frac{1}{\text{Sqrt}[17]}),$$

$$\text{Cos}[x] \to \frac{4}{\text{Sqrt}[17]}\},$$

$$\{\text{Sin}[x] \to \frac{1}{\text{Sqrt}[17]},$$

$$\text{Cos}[x] \to \frac{-4}{\text{Sqrt}[17]}\}\}$$

```
In[7]:= Solve[{9 Sin[x]^2+ 6 Cos[x] Sin[x] + Cos[x]^2==0,
           Sin[x]^2+Cos[x]^2==1}, {Sin[x],Cos[x]}]
Out[7]=
```
$$\{\{\text{Sin}[x] \to -(\frac{1}{\text{Sqrt}[10]}),$$

$$\text{Cos}[x] \to \frac{3}{\text{Sqrt}[10]}\},$$

$$\{\text{Sin}[x] \to \frac{1}{\text{Sqrt}[10]},$$

$$\text{Cos}[x] \to \frac{-3}{\text{Sqrt}[10]}\},$$

$$\{\text{Sin}[x] \to -(\frac{1}{\text{Sqrt}[10]}),$$

$$\text{Cos}[x] \to \frac{3}{\text{Sqrt}[10]}\},$$

$$\{\text{Sin}[x] \to \frac{1}{\text{Sqrt}[10]},$$

$$\text{Cos}[x] \to \frac{-3}{\text{Sqrt}[10]}\}\}$$

As can be seen, other equations can equally be solved with the method described above. For other problems in certain cases other additional equations must be provided. These equations can be taken from a table of rules. If such additional conditions are frequently needed during a *Mathematica* session, they can be defined by means of the AlgebraicRules command (see for more details [1], p. 622).

Equals sign for equations	==
To solve equation(s)	Solve[*ls* == *rs*, *var*]
To solve an equation	Roots[*ls* == *rs*, *var*]
	Roots may only be applied to an equation
To find all solutions to an equation	Reduce[*ls* == *rs*, *var*]

ls : left side of equation
rs : right side of equation
var : solution variable

With Solve and Reduce lists of equations and solution variables can be declared.

Solution of equations

4.4 Problems

1. Solve the equations $15x^2 - 2x - 8 = 0$.
2. Solve the equations $x^4 - 4x^3 = 17x^2 + 16x + 84$.
3. Solve the equations $\sqrt{(x + 2)} - 1 = \sqrt{x}$.
4. Solve the equations $2\cos^2 x + 3 \cos x + 1 = 0$.
5. Determine all solutions of the equations

$$\frac{a}{x - b} - 1 = \frac{b}{x - a}$$

as a function of a and b.

5 Linear algebra and systems of equations

5.1 Description of matrices and vectors

A matrix can be imagined as a table which, depending on one's viewpoint, consists of rows or columns. To create such tables the `Table` command is available. A 2 × 3 matrix can be produced in the following way:

```
In[1]:=Table[a[i,j],{i,1,2},{j,1,3}]
Out[1]={{a[1, 1], a[1, 2], a[1, 3]},
        {a[2, 1], a[2, 2], a[2, 3]}}
```

The *Mathematica* command `MatrixForm` produces the normal format for a matrix:

```
In[2]:=MatrixForm[%]
Out[2]=a[1, 1]    a[1, 2]    a[1, 3]
       a[2, 1]    a[2, 2]    a[2, 3]
```

From this output we can see that the first number in square brackets defines the row, while the second defines the column. As an alternative to the `Table` command the `Array` command can be used to generate matrices:

```
In[3]:=Array[a,{2,3}]
Out[3]={{a[1, 1], a[1, 2], a[1, 3]},
        {a[2, 1], a[2, 2], a[2, 3]}}
```

The output agrees with the first output. The input is somewhat shorter.

To generate diagonal matrices, the `DiagonalMatrix` command is used. The diagonal elements are input as a list:

```
In[4]:=DiagonalMatrix[{1,2,3}]
Out[4]={{1, 0, 0}, {0, 2, 0}, {0, 0, 3}}

In[5]:=MatrixForm[%]
Out[5]=1    0    0
       0    2    0
       0    0    3
```

The command `IdentityMatrix` is provided to generate the unit matrix. The

Linear algebra and systems of equations

number of diagonal elements must be given as parameter. The 2 × 2 matrix is obtained by:

```
In[6]:=IdentityMatrix[2]
Out[6]={{1, 0}, {0, 1}}
```

Because *Mathematica* manipulates matrices as lists of lists (rows), it is possible to obtain the elements of a matrix in the same way as the elements of a list. To clarify the procedure we next define a 2 × 3 matrix:

```
In[7]:=mat=Array[a,{2,3}]
Out[7]={{a[1, 1], a[1, 2], a[1, 3]},
        {a[2, 1], a[2, 2], a[2, 3]}}
```

As described in Chapter 2, the second row of the matrix (the second list input) can be obtained with the following command:

```
In[8]:=mat[[2]]
Out[8]={a[2, 1], a[2, 2], a[2, 3]}
```

The third element of the first row of the matrix is obtained by:

```
In[9]:=mat[[1,3]]
Out[9]=a[1, 3]
```

To obtain the columns of the matrix, the matrix is transposed logically (the rows and columns are swapped – that is, the first row of the transposed matrix is taken from the first column of the original matrix, and so on). The `Transpose` command performs this:

```
In[10]:=Transpose[mat]
Out[10]={{a[1, 1], a[2, 1]}, {a[1, 2], a{2, 2]},
         {a[1, 3], a[2, 3]}}
```

The second column of the output matrix is yielded by:

```
In[11]:=Transpose[mat][[2]]
Out[11]={a[1, 2], a[2, 2]}
```

In many cases a partial matrix is required. For this in *Mathematica* the matrix is called with two lists, which describe the required domain. The first list contains the description for the rows, the second that for the columns. The partial matrix, which consists of the last two columns of our matrix, is obtained by:

```
In[12]:=mat[[{1,2},{2,3}]]
Out[12]={{a[1, 2], a[1, 3]}, {a[2, 2], a[2, 3]}}
```

Vectors can be represented as single row matrices or as lists. Here it is important when providing input as a matrix to ensure that only the column number and not the row number is given. We shall say more about this in Section 5.3.

To describe a matrix	Table[$m[i,j]$, {i, $imin$, $imax$}, {j, $jmin$, $jmax$}] or Array[m, {$imax$}, {$jmax$}]
To describe a vector	Array[m, $imax$]
To transpose a matrix	Transpose[m]
Rows of a matrix	m [[i]]
Columns of a matrix	Transpose[m][[i]]
Element of a matrix	m [[i,j]]
Partial matrix	m [[{$imin$, $imax$},{$jmin$, $jmax$}]]
Diagonal matrix	DiagonalMatrix[$list$]
Unit matrix	IdentityMatrix[n]
m	:matrix
i	:row number
j	:column number
imin	:minimum row number
jmin	:minimum column number
imax	:maximum row number
jmax	:maximum column number

Matrices

5.2 Transformation of matrices

As matrices in *Mathematica* are lists, the rules for the addition and subtraction of matrices described in Chapter 3 apply. With multiplication we need to distinguish between multiplication with a scalar and the multiplication of matrices. To illustrate the commands, we shall define three matrices:

```
In[1]:=mat1=Array[a,{2,3}]
Out[1]={{a[1, 1], a[1, 2], a[1, 3]},
        {a[2, 1], a[2, 2], a[2, 3]}}

In[2]:=mat2=Array[b,{3,2}]
Out[2]={{b[1, 1], b[1, 2]}, {b[2, 1], b[2, 2]},
        {b[3, 1], b[3, 2]}}

In[3]:=mat3=Array[c,{2,3}]
Out[3]={{c[1, 1], c[1, 2], c[1,3]},
        {c[2, 1], c[2, 2], c[2, 3]}}
```

If we attempt to add matrices mat1 and mat2, we get the following error message:

```
In[4]:=mat1+mat2
Out[4]=Thread::tdlen:
    Objects of unequal length in TooBig
    cannot be combined.
        {{a[1, 1], a[1, 2], a[1, 3]},
         {a[2, 1], a[2, 2], a[2, 3]}} +
        {{b[1, 1], b[1, 2]}, {a[2, 1], b[2, 2]},
         {b[3, 1], b[3, 2]}}
```

The error message means that it is not possible to add (or subtract) matrices with unequal numbers of rows or columns. Now we sum the first and third matrix:

```
In[5]:=mat1+mat3
Out[5]={{a[1, 1] + c[1, 1], a[1, 2] + c[1, 2],
         a[1, 3] + c[1, 3]},
        {a[2, 1] + c[2, 1], a[2, 2] + c[2, 2],
         a[2, 3] + c[2, 3]}}
```

Here *Mathematica* carries out the addition correctly, as it does for subtraction.

To multiply a matrix by a number, each is separated by a blank space or the multiplication symbol:

```
In[6]:=7*mat1
Out[6]={{7 a[1, 1], 7 a[1, 2], 7 a[1, 3]},
        {7 a[2, 1], 7 a[2, 2], 7 a[2, 3]}}
```

The same result is obtained by inputting 7 mat1. This procedure is customary in mathematics. *Mathematica* can also add a number to a matrix, which is not possible in mathematics, because variable objects are involved. An example:

```
In[7]:=17+mat2
Out[7]={{17 + b[1, 1], 17 + b[1, 2]},
        {17 + b[2, 1], 17 + b[2, 2]},
        {17 + b[3, 1], 17 + b[3, 2]}}
```

This procedure is certainly convenient so far as the input is concerned, but should be used with caution.

In order to multiply matrices in *Mathematica*, the matrices are joined by a full stop (period). This multiplication follows the normal mathematical process:

```
In[8]:=mat1.mat2
Out[8]={{a[1, 1] b[1, 1] + a[1, 2] b[2, 1] +
         a[1, 3] b[3, 1], a[1, 1] b[1, 2] +
         a[1, 2] b[2, 2] + a[1, 3] b[3, 2]},
        {a[2, 1] b[1, 1] + a[2, 2] b[2, 1] +
         a[2, 3] b[3, 1], a[2, 1] b[1, 2] +
         a[2, 2] b[2, 2] + a[2, 3] b[3, 2]}}
```

For it to be possible to multiply matrices, the row length of the first matrix must agree with the column length of the second matrix. As a further example, we shall illustrate the matrix inverse of square matrices. The command is Inverse:

```
In[9]:=mat4=Array[d,{2,2}]
Out[9]={{d[1, 1], d[1, 2]}, {d[2, 1], d[2, 2]}}

In[10]:=Inverse[mat4]
Out[10]=
                     d[2, 2]
     {{-------------------------------------,
        -(d[1, 2] d[2, 1]) + d[1, 1] d[2, 2]

                       d[1, 2]
       -(-------------------------------------)},
          -(d[1, 2] d[2, 1]) + d[1, 1] d[2, 2]

                         d[2, 1]
      {-(-------------------------------------),
          -(d[1, 2] d[2, 1]) + d[1, 1] d[2, 2]

                     d[1, 1]
       -------------------------------------}}
       -(d[1, 2] d[2, 1]) + d[1, 1] d[2, 2]
```

Here we have intentionally chosen a simple example in order to preserve the readability of the output: *Mathematica* can handle more complicated examples.

Additionally, *Mathematica* also contains commands for the calculation of the eigenvalues and determinants of a matrix. The following examples show how the commands are applied for the fourth matrix:

```
In[11]:=Eigenvalues[mat4]
Out[11]={(d[1, 1] + d[2, 2] +

                    2
         Sqrt[d[1, 1]  + 4 d[1, 2] d[2, 1] -

                                     2
            2 d[1, 1] d[2, 2] + d[2, 2] ]) / 2,

        (d[1, 1] + d[2, 2] -

                    2
         Sqrt[d[1, 1]  + 4 d[1, 2] d[2, 1] -

                                     2
            2 d[1, 1] d[2, 2] + d[2, 2] ]) / 2}

In[12]:=Det[mat4]
Out[12]=-(d[1, 2] d[2, 1]) + d[1, 1] d[2, 2]
```

Even with these illustrated examples we are far from describing the full range of commands that *Mathematica* offers for matrices. Each new version of *Mathematica* comes with supplementary packages that contain many commands for the manipulation of matrices.

Linear algebra and systems of equations

Matrix addition	+
Multiplication of a matrix by a number	* or a blank space
Matrix multiplication	.
Matrix inversion for square matrices	Inverse[m]
Eigenvalues of a square matrix	Eigenvalues[m]
Determinants of a square matrix	Det[m]

Calculating with matrices

5.3 Calculating with vectors

The same rules as for matrices apply for the addition and subtraction of vectors. Similarly, vectors can be multiplied with scalars. Therefore we give only a few examples:

```
In[1]:=v1=Array[a,{3}]
Out[1]={a[1], a[2], a[3]}

In[2]:=v2=Array[b,{3}]
Out[2]={b[1], b[2], b[3]}

In[3]:=v3=Array[c,{3}]
Out[3]={c[1], c[2], c[3]}

In[4]:=v1+v2
Out[4]={a[1] + b[1], a[2] + b[2], a[3] + b[3]}

In[5].:=v1-v2
Out[5]={a[1] - b[1], a[2] - b[2], a[3] - b[3]}

In[6]:=19 v1
Out[6]={19 a[1], 19 a[2], 19 a[3]}
```

The scalar product of two vectors can be calculated using a dot (full stop), as with matrices:

```
In[7]:=v1.v2
Out[7]=a[1] b[1] + a[2] b[2] + a[3] b[3]
```

From the output, we see that the scalar product is calculated in the normal way. Because the scalar product is not associative (that is, it is

$$(\vec{x}, \vec{y})\vec{z} \neq \vec{x}(\vec{y}, \vec{z})),$$

we shall consider in the following example the scalar product v1.v2.v3:

```
In[8]:=v1.v2.v3
Out[8]=(a[1] b[1] + a[2] b[2] + a[3] b[3])
       {c[1], c[2], c[3]}
```

Mathematica first calculates v1.v2 and then tries to scalar multiply the result of the multiplication with the third vector. As this multiplication is not defined mathematically, *Mathematica* leaves the intermediate result unaltered. This illustrates why one should carefully consider whether the input is mathematically sound when multiplying vectors.

When calculating with vectors, the cross product is frequently needed. In order to calculate the cross product of two vectors with *Mathematica*, additional commands must be loaded from a supplementary package.

The following input loads these commands: <<Calculus`VectorAnalysis`

If *Mathematica* is correctly installed, the Vector Analysis.m file is located in the Calculus sub-directory. The extension .m depends on the operating system. The word VectorAnalysis must, however, be enclosed between single quotes ('). We now give two examples of calculating the cross product – first a simple one, then the cross product of the vectors v1 and v2:

```
In[9]:=CrossProduct[{1,0,0},{0,1,0}]
Out[9]={0, 0, 1}

In[10]:=CrossProduct[v1,v2]
Out[10]={-(a[3] b[2]) + a[2] b[3], a[3] b[1] - a[1] b[3],
        -(a[2] b[1] + a[1] b[2]}
```

Addition of vectors	+
Multiplication of a vector by a number	*
Scalar product	.
Cross product	CrossProduct[v1,v2]

Calculating with vectors

5.4 Solution of systems of equations

First we shall examine linear systems of equations more thoroughly, so that the solution of any systems of equations can be illustrated by means of examples.

Just as with equations, *Mathematica* allows the commands Solve and Reduce to be used for solving linear systems of equations. The only question is the method of input of the equation system. A simple possibility is to input the equations and solution variables in the form of a list. The exact form of the input

Linear algebra and systems of equations

can be seen from the following example:

```
In[1]:=Solve[{ x - 3 y -   z ==4,
              2 x +   y +  z ==3,
              3 x - 2 y - 2 z == 1},{x,y,z}]
Out[1]={{x -> 1, y -> -2, z -> 3}}
```

The next example shows a somewhat shorter method for entering the system. First the coefficient matrix of the equations system is input; this is scalar multiplied by the vector x, y, z and the result is immediately set to the result vector 4, 3, 1:

```
In[2]:=Solve[{{1,- 3, -1},{2,1,1},{3,-2,-2}}.{x,y,z}==
        {4,3,1},{x,y,z}]
Out[2]={{x -> 1, y -> 2, z -> 3}}
```

Of course, *Mathematica* can also solve equation systems in which the number of equations and variables do(es) not agree. Here are two examples:

```
In[3]:=Solve[{{5,2},{3,-1},{2,3}}.{x,y}=={5,14,-9}, {x,y}]
Out[3]={{x -> 3, y -> -5}}

In[4]:=Solve[{{2,2,-4,5},{0,0,2,-1},{1,1,1,1}}.
        {a,b,c,d}=={5,1,4},{a,b,c,d}]
Out[4]=        7        3 d         1   d
       {{a -> - - b - ---, c -> - + -}}
                2        2          2   2
```

In the previous example *b* and *d* were chosen as parameters for the solution, which is logical given the structure of the solution set.

In equation systems with parameters *Mathematica* can equally find the solutions, provided that the solution variables are input exactly:

```
In[5]:=Solve[{{1,0,t},{0,1,-1},{t,1,0}}.{x,y,z}=={4,0,3},
         {x,y,z}]
Out[5]=                              2
                  -3 + 4 t - 3 (-1 + t )            3 - 4 t
         {{x -> -(---------------------), y -> -(-------),
                              2                    2
                       t (-1 + t )                -1 + t

                  3 - 4 t
         z -> -(-------)}}
                   2
                -1 + t

In[6]:=Solve[{{1,0,t},{0,1,-1},{t,1,0}}.{x,y,z}=={4,0,3},
         {x,y,t}]
Out[6]=                          2
         {{x -> 2 - Sqrt[4 - 3 z + z ], y -> z,
```

$$t \to \dfrac{\dfrac{4}{z} + \dfrac{2\,\text{Sqrt}[4 - 3z + z^2]}{z}}{2}\Big\},$$

$$\{x \to 2 + \text{Sqrt}[4 - 3z + z^2],\ y \to z,$$

$$t \to \dfrac{\dfrac{4}{z} - \dfrac{2\,\text{Sqrt}[4 - 3z + z^2]}{z}}{2}\Big\}\Big\}$$

The last two examples show that *Mathematica* determines the solution according to how the solution variables are input. It does not, however, seek the existence of the solution for all parameter values. This task can be achieved with the Reduce command:

```
In[7]:=Reduce[{{1,0,t},{0,1,-1},{t,1,0}}.{x,y,z}=={4,0,3},
         {x,y,z}]
```
$$\text{Out[7]}= (-1 + t)\,(1 + t) \,!=\, 0 \,\&\&\, x == \dfrac{4 - 3t}{1 - t^2} \,\&\&$$
$$y == \dfrac{3 - 4t}{1 - t^2} \,\&\&\, z == \dfrac{3 - 4t}{1 - t^2}$$

Even with equation systems that place high demands on accuracy *Mathematica* finds the exact solution (see [[5]]), so that only with very large equation systems does one have to resort to approximation procedures:

```
In[8]:=Solve[{{3,4},{300000,400001}}.{x,y}=={7,700001},{x,y}]
Out[8]={{x -> 1, y -> 1}}
```

Now two examples dealing with non-linear equation systems:

```
In[9]:=Solve[{3 x^2 +4 y^2==16,4 x^2 + 3y^2==19},{x,y}]
Out[9]={{x -> 2, y -> 1}, {x -> -2, y -> 1},
        {x -> 2, y -> -1}, {x -> -2, y -> -1}}

In[10]:=Solve[{x+2 y==20,x^2+y^2==100},{x,y}]
Out[10]={{x -> 0, y -> 10}, {x -> 8, y -> 6}}
```

From these examples it can be seen that *Mathematica* is well able to solve smaller non-linear equation systems. As larger systems cannot generally be solved analytically, we have to use numerical methods for their solution, as offered by the NSolve command.

Linear algebra and systems of equations

Equals sign for equations	==
To solve systems of equations	`Solve[{ ls == rs...}, var ]`
	or
	`Solve[ m.vector, var]`
To find all solutions of a system of equations	`Reduce[ {ls == rs...}, var ]`
	or
	`Reduce[ m.vector, var ]`
ls	:left side of the equation
rs	:right side of the equation
var	:list of solution variables
m	:matrix of the system of equations
vector	:vector with the variables of the system of equations

Solution of systems of equations

5.5 Problems

Given the following matrices:

$$M_1 = \begin{pmatrix} 1 & 2 & 3 \\ 4 & 5 & 6 \\ 7 & 8 & 9 \end{pmatrix} \quad M_2 = \begin{pmatrix} 1 & 0 & 1 \\ 0 & 1 & 0 \\ 0 & 1 & 1 \end{pmatrix}$$

1. Find the sums of the matrices M_1 and M_2.
2. Find the product of the matrices M_1 and M_2.
3. Find the transposed matrix of the matrix M_1.
4. Find the determinant of the matrix M_2.
5. Find the inverse of the matrix M_2.
6. Solve the following system of equations:

$2x + 8y + 14z = 178$
$7x + y + 4z = 74$
$4x + 7y + z = 77$

6 Graphics

A powerful feature of *Mathematica* is its generation of diagrams. It is especially attractive for its ability to produce three-dimensional displays.

In this chapter we examine first two-dimensional graphics, followed by three-dimensional graphics.

6.1 2D graphics

The powerful `Plot` command is used to draw the graph of a function with *Mathematica*. The reason for the description 'powerful' is because some parameters can be passed to it and more than 40 options can be applied. A complete description of all these options is beyond the scope of this book, so we shall only describe some of the important ones. The function to be drawn and the area in which it is to be plotted are given to the `Plot` command. The following example illustrates the graph of the sine function:

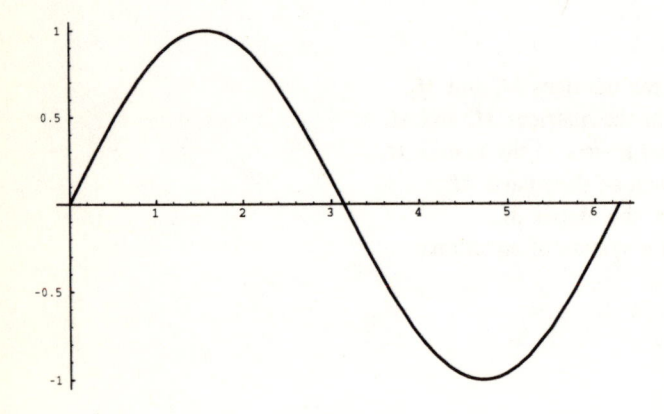

```
In[1]:=Plot[Sin[x],{x,0,2 Pi}]
Out[1]=
```

At this call of the `Plot` command *Mathematica* first checks which *x*-values are required for the plot and then evaluates the function for these *x*-values. This method is usually the quickest. Should the function first be evaluated and then the

Graphics

x-values be established, this can be done with the `Evaluate` command. The call for the previous example would then appear as follows:

```
Plot[Evaluate[Sin[x]],{x,0,2 Pi}]
```

This call is therefore logical when it is preferable to evaluate the function first. This happens, for example, with Legendre, Hermite and Laguerre polynomials.

If we want to represent the graphs of several functions in a coordinate system, the functions are given to the `Plot` command as a list, which is enclosed in curly brackets:

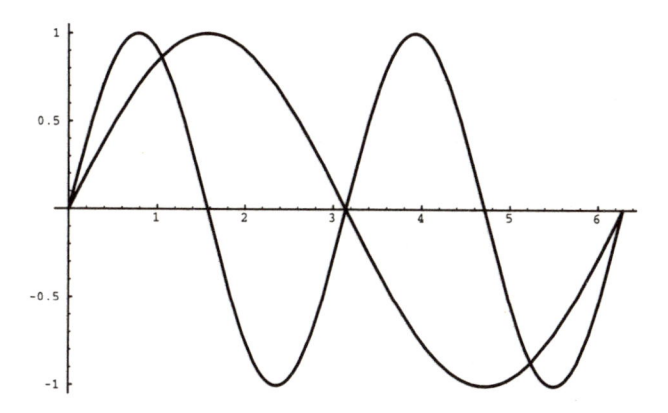

```
In[2]:=Plot[{Sin[x],Sin[2 x]},{x,0,2 Pi}]
Out[2]=
```

It is difficult to distinguish the individual graphs in this output. To facilitate interpretation, colours, different types of line and different line thicknesses are used. All of these are included in *Mathematica*. The next example shows the procedure for obtaining different thicknesses. The `Thickness` command is used here. (This is a relative instruction with regard to the total size of the drawing.) The `PlotStyle` command is used to designate the different line thicknesses for the individual functions that are specified in the first list:

```
In[3]:=Plot[{Sin[x],Sin[2 x]},{x,0,2 Pi},
            PlotStyle->{Thickness[0.005],
            Thickness[0.01]}]
Out[3]=
```

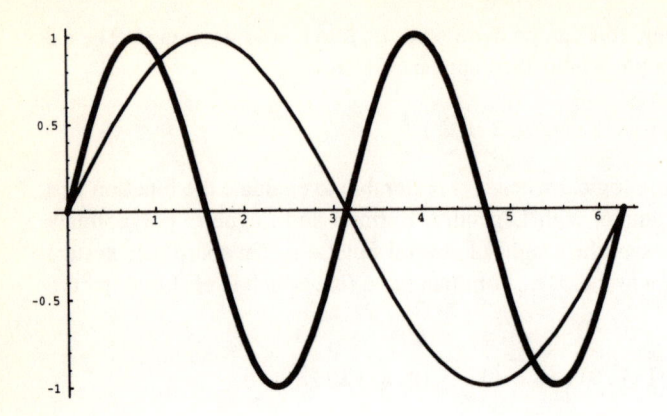

Other options available are RBGColor and Dashing for the choice of colours and types of line. The axes of the coordinate system can be labelled using the AxesLabel option. These descriptions must be enclosed within double quote marks. When AxesLabel is used, the first list given is interpreted as for the *x*-axis, while the second is for the *y*-axis.

To obtain the graphical output of previously defined data, the command Show is used:

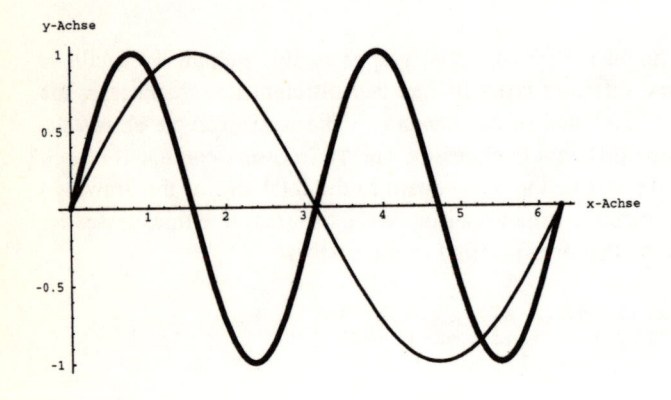

In[4]:=Show[%,AxesLabel->{"x-axis","y-axis"}]
Out[4]=

The options Frame and GridLines place the output within a frame with a background grid:

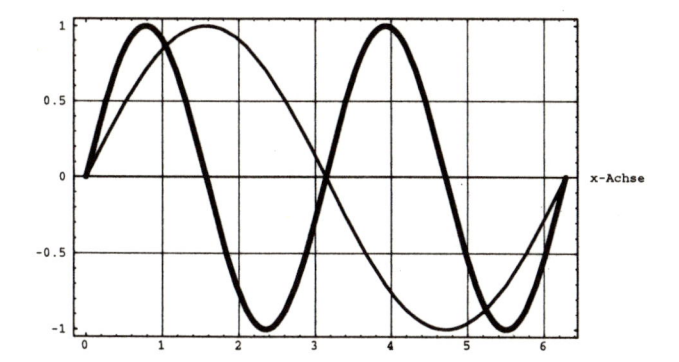

```
In[5]:=Show[%,AxesLabel->{"x-axis","y-axis"},
        Frame->True,
        Gridlines->Automatic]
Out[5]=
```

With this combination of the options the *y*-axis is not labelled. To obtain this, the option `FrameLabel` must be used instead of `AxesLabel`. Where the same scale is required for both axes, the `AspectRatio` option, set to the value 1, must be used.

6.1.1 Parameterised curves

Many applications involve parameterised curves. The command `ParametricPlot` is available to draw these curves. It is used in a similar way to `Plot`. The first example shows a logarithmic spiral:

```
In[1]:=ParametricPlot[{E^0.001 t Sin[t],E^0.001 t
                      Cos[t]}, {t,0,8 Pi}]
Out[1]=
```

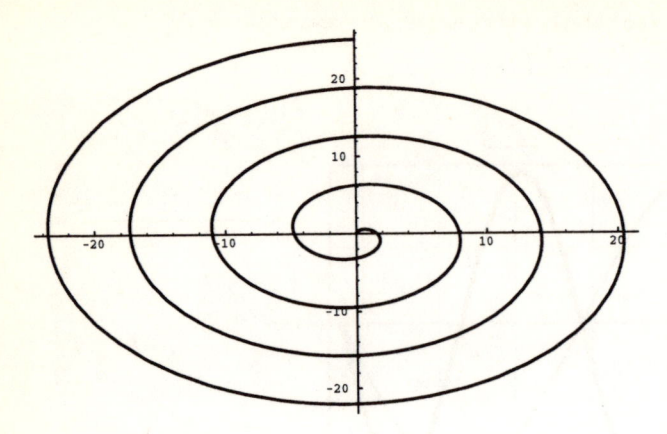

As with many other commands, a list (of parameterised curves) can be given to `ParametricPlot`.

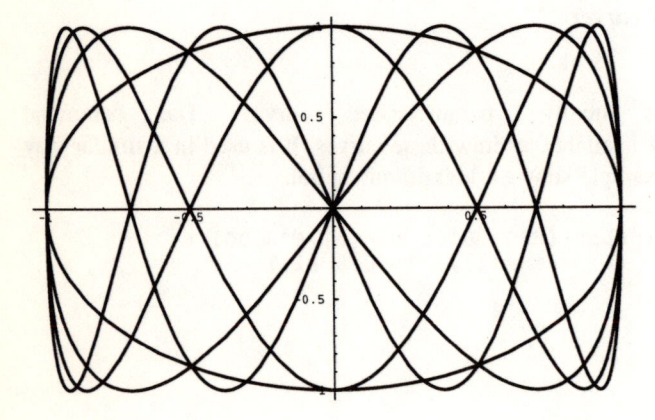

```
In[2]:=ParametricPlot[{{Cos[t],Sin[t]},
            {Cos[t],Sin[2 t]},
            {Cos[t],Sin[3 t]} ,
            {Cos[t],Sin[4 t]}},
            {t,0,2 Pi}]
Out[2]=
```

Unfortunately, the versions of *Mathematica* available to the author do not allow the list to be given directly to `ParametricPlot` using the `Table` command.

Graphics

6.1.2 Representation of tables

An application that often arises is the graphical representation of tables. To explain the procedure, we shall first define a table. Tables can also be read in from a data carrier with the aid of the `ReadList` command. The only important requirement is for each entry to consist of exactly two plottable numbers – that is, the list must contain no symbols that *Mathematica* cannot convert into decimal numbers:

```
In[1]:=table={{0,0},{1,2},{2,0},{3,-2},{4,0}}
Out[1]={{0, 0}, {1, 2}, {2, 0}, {3, -2}, {4, 0}}
```

The values of the table can be put into a graph with the `ListPlot` command. To aid readability the size of the plot points can be specified with the `PointSize` option:

```
In[2]:=ListPlot[table,PlotStyle->PointSize[0.05]]
Out[2]=
```

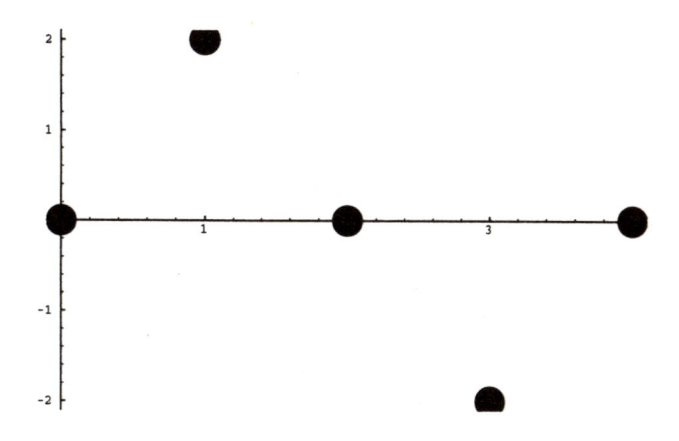

If we require the points to be joined, the `PlotJoined` option is set to `True`:

```
In[3]:=ListPlot[Table,PlotJoined->True]
Out[3]=
```

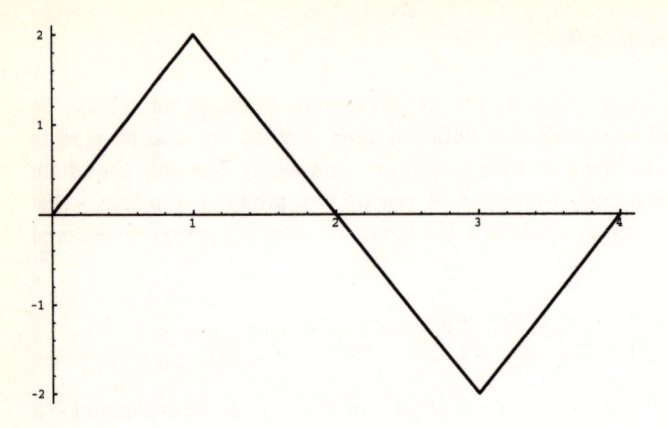

[Graph showing a triangular wave with peak at 2 and trough at -2, crossing x-axis near 0, 2, and 4]

To plot the graph of a function	Plot[*list*, {*var*, *varmin*, *varmax*}]
To obtain the evaluation of an expression	Evaluate[*expr*]
To set the plot style	PlotStyle->
To specify line thickness	Thickness[*r*]
To specify point size	PointSize[*r*]
To label axes	AxesLabel -> ...
To frame a plot	Frame -> True
To plot parameterised curves	ParametricPlot[*list*, {*var*, *varmin*, *varmax*}]
To plot lists	ListPlot[*table*]
To join up points	PlotJoined -> True
To display a plot	Show[*graphic*]

list   :list of functions
var   :variable descriptor
varmin :smallest value for the variable
varmax :largest value for the variable
r   :fractional size of line thickness in relation to the total size of the plot
graphic :list, consisting of graphics elements

2-D graphics

6.2 3D-graphics

This section first describes the `Plot3D` command which is required to draw three-dimensional graphics. It is equivalent to the `Plot` command in the plane, and it has similarly a large number of options, a selection of which will be presented in due course.

A function term with two variables, together with the domains of both variables, must be given to the `Plot3D` command:

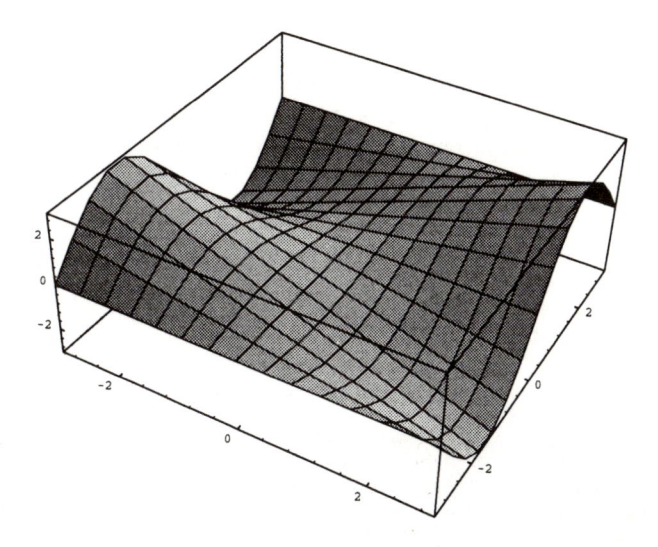

```
In[1]:=Plot3D[x Sin[y],{x,-3,3},{y,-Pi,Pi}]
Out[1]=
```

If we want to view the diagram from a point different from that originally given, this can be done with the `ViewPoint` option. The three coordinates of the viewpoint are enclosed within curly brackets and arranged in order by prefixing with an arrow (->). In the next example the previous diagram is viewed from the direction of the *x*-axis:

```
In[2]:=Plot3D[x Sin[y],{x,-3,3},{y,-Pi,Pi},
        ViewPoint->{3.4,0,0}]
Out[2]=
```

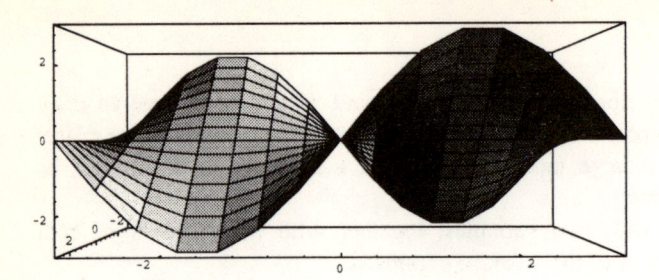

If the connecting lines appear too angular, the number of points per line (`PlotPoints`) can be increased. Of course, this is possible only at the expense of memory space and time, though the results often repay these costs. The following example shows the results from plotting 50 points per line:

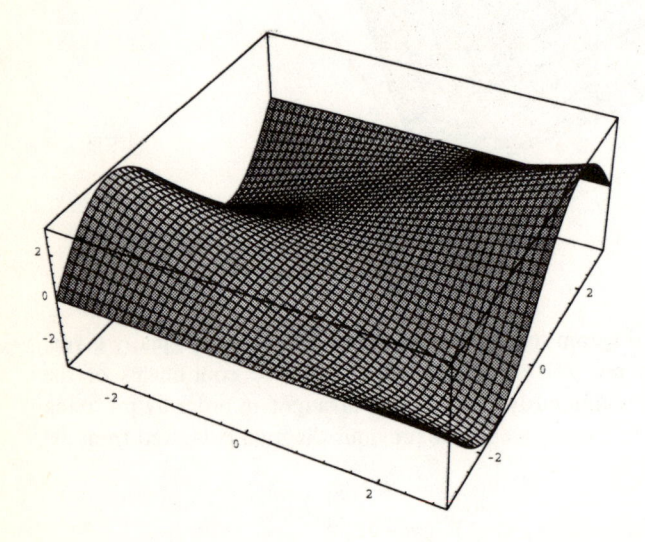

```
In[3]:=Plot3D[x Sin[y],{x,-3,3},{y,-Pi,Pi},
       PlotPoints->50]
Out[3]=
```

Here the connection points are much smoother. However, too many lines in a diagram can be counterproductive. In this case the option `Mesh` can be set to `False`, in order to emphasise the representation of the grid lines:

Graphics

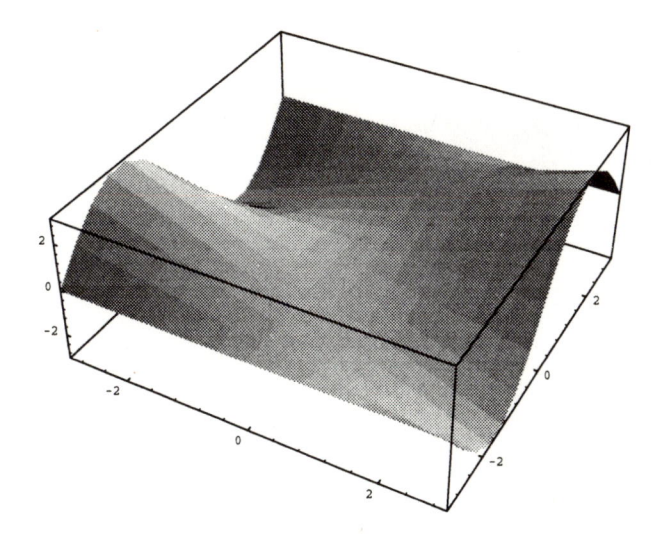

```
In[4]:=Plot3D[x Sin[y],{x,-3,3},{y,-Pi,Pi},
        Mesh->False]
Out[4]=
```

If we want to combine two or more graphics in a diagram, these cannot be given as a list to the Plot3D command, because it only accepts a function. Therefore, the different graphics must first be produced and then joined with the Show command. To illustrate the procedure, we shall first produce another graphic. This and the previous graphic will then be shown together in one diagram:

```
In[5]:=Plot3D[x Cos[y],{x,-3,3},{y,-Pi,Pi},
            Mesh->False]
Out[5]=
```

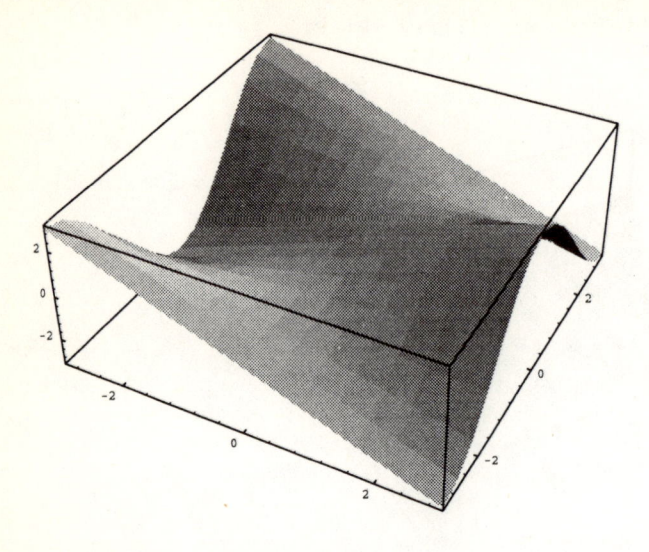

```
In[6]:=Show[%,%%]
Out[6]=
```

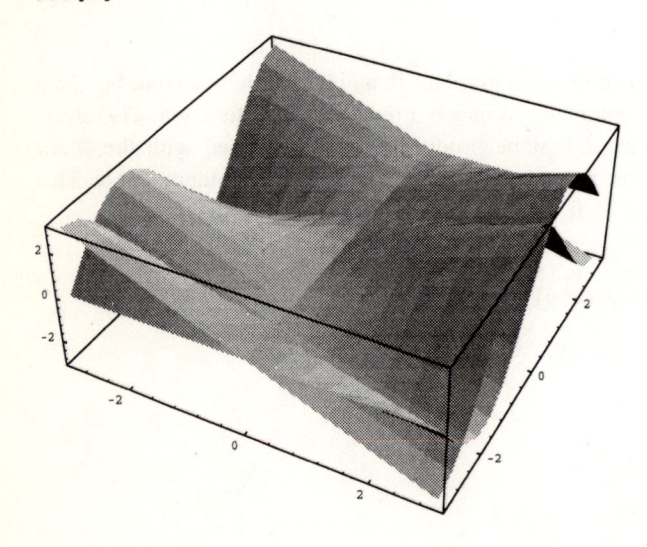

A further powerful command for representing parameterised diagrams in space is ParametricPlot3D. This command allows both parameterised curves and surfaces to be represented in space. In the next two examples the command is used to draw a cylinder and a sphere:

Graphics 59

```
In[7]:=ParametricPlot3D[{Cos[t],Sin[t],u},{t,0,2 Pi},
                        {u,-2,2}]
Out[7]=
```

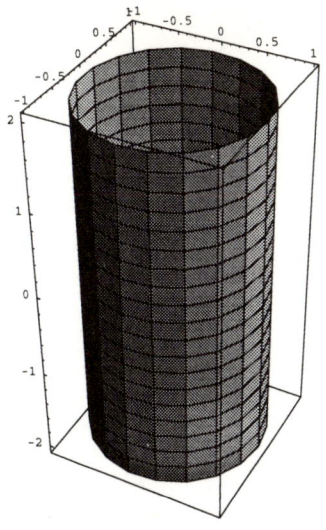

```
In[8]:=ParametricPlot3D[{2 Cos[u] Cos[t],
                         2 Cos[u] Sin[t],2 Sin[u]},
                        {t,0,2 Pi},{u,-Pi/2,Pi/2}]
Out[8]=
```

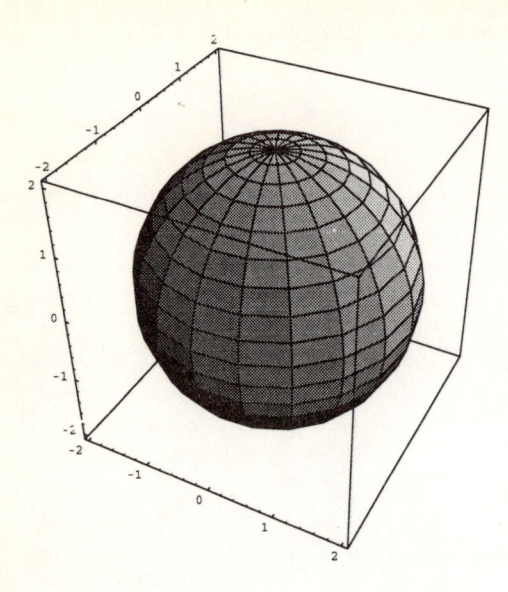

To include the last two graphics in a single diagram, we can use the Show command, as described above. The other possibility is to pass a list of the graphics to the ParametricPlot3D command. With this method, however, the parameters for all graphics are selected at the same time. The implication for the user is either that more calculation is required for some parameters or that part of the drawing is changed. For this reason, invoking the Show command is often simpler:

In[9]:=Show[%,%%]
Out[9]=

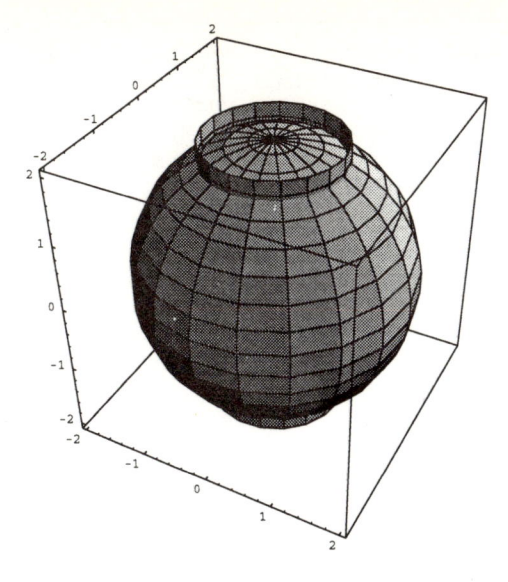

The examples included here reveal only a small range of the graphics facilities offered by *Mathematica*. Other facilities include:

- List graphics with and without error bars
- Pie charts and bar charts
- Animation

This list can be extended. Additional facilities will be found in the latest versions of the software.

To plot the diagram of a function	`Plot3D[ f,`
	`{var1, var1min, var1max}`
	`{var2, var2min, var2max} ]`

To fix an observer's viewpoint	`ViewPoint ->{x,y,z}`
To set the number of points in a curve	`PlotPoints -> number` (Default value 25)
To hide the base grid	`Mesh -> False`

To draw parameterised curves or surfaces	`ParametricPlot3D`
	`[ functions list,`
	`{var1, var1min, var1max},`
	`{var2, var2min, var2max} ]`

To display graphics	`Show [graphic ]`

f	:function with two variables
functions list	:list of functions
var	:variable descriptor
varmin	:smallest value for the variable
varmax	:largest value for the variable
graphic	:list, consisting of graphics elements

3D graphics

6.3 Problems

1. Plot the diagram of function *f* with

$$f(x) = \frac{\sin x}{x}$$

between 0.001 and 2π with labelled frame and a grid pattern in the background.
2. Plot a semicircle with radius 2.
3. Plot a hemisphere with radius 2.

7 Analysis

Computer-based algebra systems like *Mathematica* are a useful and valuable aid for many tasks in analysis; they also save time and even make some tasks in analysis worth attempting. We cannot describe the whole spectrum of applications here, but in the following sections we shall examine a selection of the commands offered by *Mathematica* for the solution of problems in analysis.

7.1 Derivatives

Mathematica provides the D command for differentiating of functions. It enables both the derivative of a function of one variable and the partial derivative of a several variables to be determined. Since the D command has several uses, both the function, and, separated by a comma, the variable with respect to which it is to be differentiated, must be specified. First of all we will give two simple examples:

```
In[1]:=D[x^n,x]
Out[1]=       -1 + n
          n x

In[2]:=D[a x^n,a]
Out[2]=    n
          x
```

In the first example x^n is derived for x; in the second ax^n for a. Next, we give a couple of examples that illustrate *Mathematica*'s ability to handle functions of one variable:

```
In[3]:=D[Log[t^2-x^2],x]
Out[3]= -2 x
        -------
          2   2
         t - x

In[4]:=D[3 Sqrt[Cos[1-x^2]],x]
Out[4]=              2
           3 x Sin[1 - x ]
         -------------------
                          2
          Sqrt[Cos[1 - x ]]
```

```
In[5]:=D[E^Tan[x],x]
Out[5]= Tan[x]    2
       E      Sec[x]
```

The example can be pursued further. In many applications, not only the first, but higher derivatives of the function are required. This can be achieved by bracketing the D command an appropriate number of times. But *Mathematica* offers a simpler way of writing the command:

```
In[6]:=D[E^Tan[x],{x,3}]
Out[6]=
       Tan[x]      4    Tan[x]      6
    2 E       Sec[x]  + E       Sec[x]  +

       Tan[x]      4              Tan[x]      2       2
    6 E       Sec[x]  Tan[x] + 4 E       Sec[x]  Tan[x]
```

With this form of input, the variable of differentiation and the required derivation must be enclosed within curly brackets and be given to the D command as second argument.

Also, the frequently used f' description for the derivation of a function is available in *Mathematica*. To illustrate the procedure, we first define a function:

```
In[7]:=f[x_]:=Log[x^2-x+1]/6+
            ArcTan[(2 x-1)/Sqrt[3]]/Sqrt[3]-Log[x+1]/3
```

Now the derivative:

```
In[8]:=f'[x]
Out[8]=    -1              -1 + 2 x                    2
        ---------   +   ---------------   +   ---------------------
         3 (1 + x)                2                            2
                         6 (1 - x + x )                (-1 + 2 x)
                                               3 (1 + -----------)
                                                           3
```

Because this term is still rather large, it is simplified in the next line:

```
In[9]:=Together[Simplify[%]]
Out[9]=   x
        ------
             3
        1 + x
```

Hitherto we have introduced examples that have illustrated numerous applications. But *Mathematica* is capable of even more. The following example will give an impression of these capabilities:

```
In[10]:=D[Log[g[x]]^8,{x,2}]
Out[10]=
          56 Log[g[x]]^6 g'[x]^2     8 Log[g[x]]^7 g'[x]^2
          ---------------------  -   ---------------------  +
                 g[x]^2                     g[x]^2

          8 Log[g[x]]^7 g''[x]
          --------------------
                 g[x]
```

This output shows that *Mathematica* can also implement the rules of differentiation for indefinite functions.

We can also see how partial derivatives are determined from some of these examples, depending upon the viewpoint. We shall show other applications. First the determination of

$$\frac{\partial(x^2 - y^2)}{\partial x}$$

```
In[11]:=D[x^2-y^2,x]
Out[11]=2 x
```

Here we have determined for *x*. Now

$$\frac{\partial(x^2 - y^2)}{\partial x \partial y}$$

```
In[12]:=D[x^2-y^2,x,y]
Out[12]=0
```

Because the derivation for *x* contains no *y*, *Mathematica* yields the correct result 0.

In the next example we consider the same derivations for the function *f* with

$$f(x,y) = e^x \cos y + \sqrt{x^2 - y^2}$$

```
In[13]:=D[E^x Cos[y] + Sqrt[x^2-y^2],x]
Out[13]=       x
         -------------  + E^x Cos[y]
         Sqrt[x^2 - y^2]

In[14]:=D[E^x Cos[y] + Sqrt[x^2-y^2],x,y]
Out[14]=    x y
         -----------  - E^x Sin[y]
         (x^2 - y^2)^{3/2}
```

To calculate the total differential of a function, there is the Dt command. The procedure is to input after the Dt command the function term separated by a comma from the variable for which the total derivative is to be obtained. The total differential for *xy*:

```
In[15]:=Dt[x y]
Out[15]=y Dt[x] + x Dt[y]
```

The total derivative of *xy* with respect to *x*:

```
In[16]:=Dt[x y,x]
Out[16]=y + x Dt[y, x]
```

Now the same for a more complicated function term:

```
In[17]:=Dt[x/Sqrt[x^2-y^2]]
Out[17]=    Dt[x]          x (2 x Dt[x] - 2 y Dt[y])
         -------------  -  --------------------------
              2   2                2    2 3/2
          Sqrt[x - y ]         2 (x  - y )

In[18]:=Dt[x/Sqrt[x^2-y^2],x]
Out[18]=     1             x (2 x - 2 y Dt[y, x])
         -------------  -  ----------------------
              2   2                2    2 3/2
          Sqrt[x - y ]         2 (x  - y )
```

The output shows how *Mathematica* also allows for the fact that *y* can depend on *x* (Dt[y,x]).

Derivative of a function	D[*f*, *var*]
	or *f*'[*var*]
Multiple derivative of a function	D[*f*, {*var*, *number*}]
Partial derivative of a function	D[*f*, {*var* ...}]
Total derivative of a function	Dt[*f*]
Total derivative of a function with respect to a variable	Dt[*f*, *var*]
f :function	
var :variable, for which it is to be derived	
number :number of derivatives	

Derivatives

7.2 Integrals

The Integrate command is used for the analytical determination of integrals.

Analysis

The first argument given to it is a function term in one or more variables. The integration variables are then added, separated by a comma.

First we shall look at some examples from one-dimensional analysis for the determinination of indefinite integrals, which are also often described as antiderivatives:

```
In[1]:=Integrate[Sin[x],x]
Out[1]=-Cos[x]

In[2]:=Integrate[x/(x^3+1),x]
Out[2]=           -1 + 2 x                                         2
          ArcTan[--------]
                 Sqrt[3]      Log[1 + x]   Log[1 - x + x ]
         ----------------  -  ----------  + ----------------
              Sqrt[3]             3                6
```

This example was considered in the previous section.

To determine surfaces that include the curves between 1 and 10, a list is given as second argument to the `Integrate` command, consisting of integration variable (here *x*), lower limit (here 1) and upper limit (here 10):

```
In[3]:=Integrate[x/x^3+1),{x,1,10}]
Out[3]=
                1                   19
         ArcTan[-------]      ArcTan[-------]
                Sqrt[3]              Sqrt[3]       Log[2]    Log[11]
       -(----------------)  + ----------------  +  ------  - -------  +
              Sqrt[3]              Sqrt[3]            3         3

         Log[91]
         -------
            6
```

The output shows the exact solution. The decimal approximation is obtained with N:

```
In[4]:=N[%]
Out[4]=0.735674
```

Mathematica also allows the calculation of improper integrals (that is, integrals in which one or both limits assume infinite values):

```
In[5]:=Integrate[1/x^2,{x,1,Infinity}]
Out[5]=1
```

However, there are also two indefinite integrals that cannot be calculated analytically. The next example shows that *Mathematica* leaves these indefinite integrals unaltered:

```
In[6]:=Integrate[E^(x^4),x]
Out[6]=     4
           x
  Integrate[E  , x]
```

When we nevertheless require a surface, we use the NIntegrate command. The syntax of this command is the same as for the determination of finite (definite) integrals. The output is, however, always given as a decimal number:

```
In[7]:=NIntegrate[E^(x^4),{x,-2,2}]
Out[7]=584926.
```

We can calculate determinate multiple integrals. The syntax corresponds to that for the calculation of determinate integrals. Here is an example:

```
In[8]:=Integrate[x Sin[y],{x,0,1},{y,0,Pi/2}]
Out[8]=1
       -
       2
```

Indefinite integral of a function	Integrate[*f*, *var*]
Definite integral of a function	Integrate{*f*,{*var*, *varmin*, *varmax*}]
Multiple determinate integral of a function	Integrate[*f*,{*var1*, *var1min*, *var1max*}{*var2*, *var2min*, *var2max*}]
Numerical integral of a function	NIntegrate[*f*,{*var*, *varmin*, *varmax*}]

f	:function
var	:variable for which one integrates
varmin	:lower bound
varmax	:upper bound

Integral calculus

7.3 Limits, series and products

In many cases the calculation of limits demands greater effort than the theory would lead one to expect. The *Mathematica* facility for this is the Limit command. The term given as the first argument is the one whose limit is to be considered; the second argument is the variable that tends towards a value:

```
In[1]:=Limit[x^2,x->1]
Out[1]=1
```

Analysis

Now some more complicated examples:

```
In[2]:=Limit[x^2 Cos[1/x],x->0]
Out[2]=0

In[3]:=Limit[Log[x^2]/Sqrt[x],x->Infinity]
Out[3]=0

In[4]:=Limit[Sin[x]/x,x->0]
Out[4]=1

In[5]:=Limit[(a^x-b^x)/x,x->0]
Out[5]=Log[a] - Log[b]
```

The calculation of these limits with *Mathematica* is very easy and takes place incredibly quickly. In addition, the Sum command is introduced for the calculation of finite sums. The term to be summed is given as first argument; the second argument is a list that contains the summation variable, its lower and upper value plus an optional increment by which the variable is to be increased. Thus

$$\sum_{1}^{20} i:$$

```
In[6]:=Sum[i{i,1,20}]
Out[6]=210
```

$$\sum_{1}^{n} i:$$

```
In[7]:=Sum[i,{i,1,n}]
Out[7]=Sum[i, {i, 1, n}]
```

The last example shows that *Mathematica* only calculates with numerical values; it does not evaluate analytically.

The Sum command can be used, for example, to produce polynomials:

```
In[8]:=Sum[x^(2 i)/i^2,{i,1,4}]
Out[8]=
          4    6    8
     2   x    x    x
    x + -- + -- + --
         4    9    16
```

Just as one can calculate sums, one can also calculate products, using the Product command. The syntax is similar down to the interval option.

$$\prod_{1}^{10} i :$$

```
In[9]:=Product[i,{i,1,10}]
Out[9]=3628800
```

$$\prod_{1}^{3}(x + i)^2 :$$

```
In[10]:=Product[(x+i)^2,{i,1,3}]
Out[10]=      2       2       2
        (1 + x)  (2 + x)  (3 + x)
```

Finally, in this section we introduce the Series command for calculating power series. As first argument the command expects the term to be expanded; as second a list containing the variable with respect to which the expansion is to be made; as third the value about which it is to be expanded; and as fourth the highest power of the expansion variable. As an example we introduce the sine series from the null to the fifth power:

```
In[11]:=Series[Sin[x],{x,0,5}]
Out[11]=     3    5
            x    x       6
       x - -- + --- + O[x]
            6   120
```

In many cases, with these power series one can calculate as with functions – that is, differentiate, integrate, etc.:

```
In[12]:=D[%,x]
Out[12]=     2    4
            x    x       5
       1 - -- + -- + O[x]
            2   24
```

```
In[13]:=Integrate[%,x]
Out[13]=     3    5
            x    x       6
       x - -- + --- + O[x]
            6   120
```

As a last example here is the expansion of the logarithmic function from the first to the third power:

```
In[14]:=Series[Log[x],{x,1,3}]
Out[14]=                2          3
                 (-1 + x)   (-1 + x)           4
       (-1 + x) - -------- + -------- + O[-1 + x]
                    2          3
```

Analysis

Limits of a term	`Limit[term, var -> var0]`
Finite sum	`Sum[term,{var, varmin, varmax, dx}]`
Finite product	`Product[term, {var, varmin, varmax}]`
Power series	`Series[f, {var, var0, varh}]`

f	:function
term	:function term
var	:variable
varmin	:lower bound
varmax	:upper bound
var0	:fixed location for the variable
varh	:highest power of the variable
dx	:interval

Limits, sums and products

7.4 Differential equations

Much has been, and will be, written about the solution of differential equations. Even the possibilities offered by *Mathematica* are sufficient for one or more books, because *Mathematica* contains one command for the analytical solution and one for the numerical solution of differential equations. In this section we shall show some examples of how simple linear differential equations can be solved with *Mathematica*.

The command used is `DSolve`; its syntax is similar to that of `Solve`. To solve the equation $f'(x) = kf(x)$:

```
In[1]:=DSolve[f'[x]==k f[x],f[x],x]
Out[1]=
              k x
        {{f[x] -> E    C[1]}}
```

This produces the expected solution $f(x) = c_1 e^{kx}$. If we want to solve the equation for a fixed starting value (say 17), this start condition can be given to `DSolve` as a further equation:

```
In[2]:=DSolve[{f'[x]==k f[x], f[0]==17},f[x],x]
Out[2]=
                     k x
        {{f[x] -> 17 E    }}
```

As can be seen from this input, the `DSolve` expects three arguments: first a list with differential equations, then a list with the functions to be found, and as the third argument the independent variable (for all functions and derivatives it must be the same). Up to this point the style `f[x]` has always been adopted when entering the solution functions. The x in square brackets can now be omitted. The effect of this can be seen in the following input for the previous example:

```
In[3]:=DSolve[{f'[x]==k f[x], f[0]==17},f,x]
Out[3]=              k #1
         {{f -> (17 E      & )}}
```

Here the solution function *f* is output in the language of *Mathematica* as a pure function. This is described by *Mathematica* in this case through the declaration of the function body (function term), which is delimited to the right by a & sign. The variables are here shown with a # sign. This notation is convenient for advanced work with *Mathematica* because it is close to the inner structure of *Mathematica*. At the same time, because it is less readable, it should only be adopted by experienced users.

For the above reason, we shall continue to input the solution function in the f[x] form.

In the next example the differential equation is considered for a damped oscillation:

```
In[4]:=DSolve[m f''[x]+r f'[x] +k f[x]==0,f[x],x]
Out[4]=                         C[1]
         {{f[x] -> ------------------------------------ +
                                           2
                    ((r + Sqrt[-4 k m + r ]) x)/(2 m)
                   E

                                      2
              ((-r + Sqrt[-4 k m + r ]) x)/(2 m)
             E                                          C[2]}}
```

The solution is calculated correctly as the sum of two *e*-functions, in which the exponents of the *e*-functions may be complex. The next example examines the differential equation of a forced oscillation:

```
In[5]:=DSolve[m f''[x]+r f'[x] +k f[x]==a Sin[b x], f[x],x]
Out[5]=
                              C[1]
{{f[x] -> ------------------------------------ +
                                  2
            ((r + Sqrt[-4 k m + r ]) x)/(2 m)
           E

                              2
       ((-r + Sqrt[-4 k m + r ]) x)/(2 m)
      E                                    C[2] +

     (a Integrate[(-((Power[E,

                                         2
              r      Sqrt[-4 k m + r ]
         -((-(-) + ------------------) DSolve't)
              m            m
         ---------------------------
                       2
```

Analysis

```
                           2
         r     Sqrt[-4 k m + r ]
     -(-(-) + ------------------)
        m            m
     ------------------------------
                  2
                              2
         r     Sqrt[-4 k m + r ]
      -(-) + ------------------
        m            m
     ------------------------------) Dsolve't +
                  2
                              2
         r     Sqrt[-4 k m + r ]
      (-(-) - ------------------] x
        m            m
     ------------------------------] m) /
                  2
                  2
    Sqrt[-4 k m + r ]) +
  (Power[E,
                              2
         r     Sqrt[-4 k m + r ]
     -((-(-) + ------------------) DSolve't)
        m            m
     ------------------------------------ +
                  2
                              2
         r     Sqrt[-4 k m + r ]
      (-(-) - ------------------) x
        m            m
     ------------------------------ +
                  2
                              2
         r     Sqrt[-4 k m + r ]
     -(-(-) - ------------------)
        m            m
   (------------------------------ +
                  2
                              2
         r     Sqrt[-4 k m + r ]
      -(-) + ------------------
        m            m
     ------------------------------) x] m) /
                  2
                  2
    Sqrt[-4 k m + r ]) Sin[b DSolve't],
  {DSolve't, 0, x}]) / m}}
```

This output is difficult both to read and to understand. As expected, the first two terms are the solutions of the homogeneous equation; the last term consists of an integral of several *e*-functions (Power[E, ...]). The term DSolve't of this integral suggests that *Mathematica* attempts to parametrise the solution, but fails. Why *Mathematica* does not here provide a term of the form $K \sin(ax + c)$ – as would be done in a paper calculation – cannot be explained.

If you attempt to check this calculation, plan your time carefully. This example, calculated on a 386 PC with coprocessor, running at 25 MHz with *Mathematica* version 2.1 for Windows, took several hours to complete.

Mathematica also offers a command for the numerical solution of differential equations. Its syntax agrees with that of `NDSolve`. However, because the application of this command requires even more experience of differential equations and the interpretation of their solutions, we refer interested readers to the *Mathematica* handbook ([1], p. 696).

Equals sign for differential equations	`==`
To solve differential equations	`DSolve[{ls == rs...}, f[var], var]`
ls	:left side of equation
rs	:right side of equation
f	:function sought or list of sought functions
var	:independent solution variable

Solution of differential equations

7.5 Problems

1. Find the derivative:

$$\frac{d(\cos y e^{4-x^2})}{dx}$$

2. Find the partial derivative with respect to x and y:

$$\frac{\partial(\sin x e^{4-x^2})}{\partial x \partial y}$$

3. Find the indefinite integral:

$$\int \sqrt{x^2 - 2x + 5}\ dx$$

4. Find the definite integral:

$$\int_0^5 \sqrt{x^2 - 2x + 5}\ dx$$

Also, obtain a decimal approximation for the integral.

5. Solve the differential equation

$$f'(x) - x^2(f(x))^2 = x^2$$

8 Simple programs

In this chapter we shall not present a comprehensive guide to building giant program packages, but try to show by means of some simple examples how to make everyday working with *Mathematica* a little easier. First, we shall show what is meant by rule-based programming in *Mathematica*. Then we shall show how these methods may be applied to adapt *Mathematica* commands to one's own requirements, followed by a section on procedural programming in *Mathematica*.

8.1 Rule-based programming

Many mathematical problems can only be solved through the application of strict rules. In rule-based programming the program accordingly consists of a sequence of the required rules. A classic example of this procedure is the determination of the derivative of a function. Here, it is not necessary to reproduce the complete differentiation command, but rather, a command that is capable of differentiating simple rational integral and trigonometric functions. The rules that are required are as follows:

1. $(f + g)' = f' + g'$
2. $(c \cdot f)' = c \cdot f'$, if c is a constant
3. $(c)' = 0$, if c is a constant
4. $(x^n)' = n \cdot x^{n-1}$
5. $(\sin x)' = \cos x$
6. $(\cos x)' = -\sin x$

The new command is called Derivation. The transposition of the rules occurs as with the definition of functions. Thus the following definition emerges for the first rule for the derivation variable x:

```
In[1]:=Derivation[f_+g_,x ]:=Derivation[f,x]+Derivation[g,x]
```

A test for this rule:

```
In[2]:=Derivation[x^3+x,x]
Out[2]=
                                     3
         Derivation[x, x] + Derivation[x , x]
```

Simple programs

The results derives from rule (1), except that *Mathematica* arranges the terms as increasing powers of *x*, according to its normal practice. In order to program the second rule, we need a command that tests whether *c* is a constant. The command is called `FreeQ[c,x]`.

Now the second rule:

```
In[3]:=Derivation[c_ f_,x_]:=c Derivation[f,x]
       /;  FreeQ[c,x]
```

The `/;` symbol is to be interpreted as 'on condition that'.

The third rule:

```
In[4]:=Derivation[c_,x_]:=0/; FreeQ[c,x]
```

Now comes a test for the first three values:

```
In[5]:=Derivation[2 x^3+7 x^2+1,x]
Out[5]=         2                    3
       7 Derivation[x , x] + 2 Derivation[x , x]
```

After this test has proved successful the fourth rule is added in order to differentiate rational integral functions:

```
In[6]:=Derivation[x_^n_,x_]:=n x (n-1)
```

This command should now be able to calculate correctly the derivation of the function in the previous example:

```
In[7]:=Derivation[2 x^3+7 x^2+1,x]
Out[7]=              2
       14 x + 6 x
```

As can be seen, the result is correct. We will now give the rules for the trigonometric functions:

```
In[8]:=Derivation[Sin[x_],x_]:=Cos[x]
In[9]:=Derivation[Cos[x_],x_]:=-Sin[x]
```

After all the listed rules are input, some test examples are given:

```
In[10]:=Derivation[x^3+17 x+3 Sin[x],x]
Out[10]=   2
        3 x  + 17 Derivation[x, x] + 3 Cos[x]
```

In this example *x* is not derived, because there is no rule available for it. However, this rule can easily be added:

```
In[11]:=Derivation[x_,x_]:=1

In[12]:=Derivation[x^3+17 x+3 Sin[x],x]
Out[12]=         2
         17 + 3 x  + 3 Cos[x]
```

Now the result appears as expected. Here are the derivatives of further functions:

```
In[13]:=Derivation[4 x^7+5 Sin[x],x]
Out[13]=     6
         28 x  + 5 Cos[x]

In[14]:=Derivation[4 x^7+5x Sin[x],x]
Out[14]=     6
         28 x  + 5 Derivation[x Sin[x], x]
```

The last example shows that the product rule is missing. This can be expanded from the model above. By defining further rules this rule can be built up to the full scope of the D command. This approach would of course not be logical, because the command already exists.

If, however, a rule should be missing, the following section shows how the required rule can be produced.

8.2 Altering commands

Because the command for the absolute value of a number causes difficulties when solving such equations, we shall show how these can be overcome. Problems occurred, for example, in Section 4.2 with the equation $|x^2 - 10x + 20| = 4$. If we wish to use the identity described there $|x| = \sqrt{x^2}$ for real x, we can add this rule. To prevent *Mathematica*'s commands from being inadvertently altered, they are protected. This protection must be removed by the Unprotect command.

```
In[1]:=Unprotect[Abs]
Out[1]={Abs}
```

Now the new rule is added:

```
In[2]:=Abs[x_]:=Sqrt[x^2]
```

We must now protect the altered command once again with the Protect command:

```
In[3]:=Protect[Abs]
Out[3]={Abs}
```

Now, when solving the equation, the difficulties should not recur:

```
In[4]:=Solve[Abs[x^2-10 x +20]==4,x,
            VerifySolutions->True]
Out[4]={{x -> 8}, {x -> 2}, {x -> 6}, {x -> 4}}
```

> To alter commands, the procedure is as follows:
>
> 1. Unprotect the command (`Unprotect`)
> 2. Input the new rules
> 3. Protect the command (`Protect`)

Altering commands

When altering commands great care must be taken; one must know the full range of the command and all arguments in order to avoid any undesirable side-effects. As the `Abs` command can also be used for complex numbers, the alteration described above leads to problems, as can be seen from the following example:

```
In[5]:=Abs[4 + 3 I]
Out[5]=4 + 3 I
```

This value is false; it was, however, brought about by the above alteration. As this false result was caused by the rule $|x| = \sqrt{x^2}$, this rule is missing from the original definition of the sum command in *Mathematica*. When one is not quite sure about altering, one should not take the original name, but choose a new name – say, Sum in this case.

8.3 Procedural programs

In many tasks with *Mathematica* we have to input a sequence of commands again and again, in order to obtain the required result. In such cases it would be advantageous to link this sequence of commands to a new command. How this can be done will be illustrated through the discussion of curves that many readers will remember from their schooldays. In the discussion of curves the following steps are repeated:

1. Determination of derivatives
2. Search for roots of the derivative and where necessary investigation of maxima, minima and turning points
3. Declaration of the anti-derivative
4. Graph of the function on a given interval produced.

All these points must be input separately in *Mathematica*. It is, however, much simpler to link these commands into a procedure (a block) under a new name. We choose the name kd. As no parameter was given in the description above up to the interval limits (*a,b*), only these values are given. In *Mathematica* the Block command can be used to link the single commands together. First, a list with variables must be given to the command; these local variables will only be used within this block. If no local variables are required, the list remains empty. The list is followed by a comma, after which come the commands, each separated by a semicolon. To make the program more understandable when running, the Print command is used here. When the same text should be output, as a string constant, the text is enclosed within double quote marks. (The *Mathematica* Print command closely resembles the Print command in many versions of BASIC.)

```
In[1]:=kd[a_,b_]:=

        Block[{ },
            Print["The 1st derivative is :", f'[x]];
            Print["The 2nd derivative is :",f''[x]];
            Print["The 3rd derivative is :",f'''[x]];
            Print["The zero positions are :",
                    Solve[f[x]==0,x]];
            Print["The positions with f'(x)=0 sind :",
                    Solve[f'[x]==0,x]];
            Print["The positions with f''(x)=0 sind :",
                    Solve[f''[x]==0,x]];
            Print["The stem function of f is :",
                    Integrate[f[x], x]];
            Plot[f[x],{x,a,b}]
            ]
```

In order to apply the kd command, another function *f* is defined. The interval bounds (−3, 3) are passed as parameters:

```
In[2]:=f[x_]:=x^3-x

In[3]:kd[-3,3]
Out[3]:=
                              2
The 1st derivation is :-1 + 3 x
The 2nd derivation is :6 x
The 3rd derivation is :6
The zero positions are :{{x -> 1}, {x -> -1}, {x -> 0}}
The positions with f'(x)=0 are :
              1                  1
 {{x -> -------},  {x -> -(-------)}}
         Sqrt[3]            Sqrt[3]

The positions with f''(x)=0 are :{{x -> 0}}
                                 2    4
                                -x   x
The stem function of f is :--- + --
                                 2    4
```

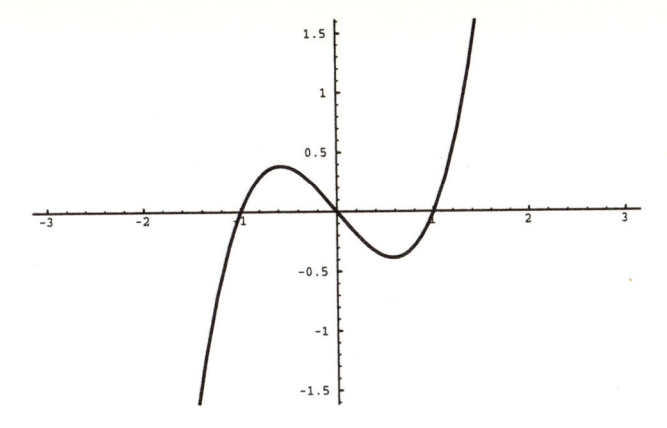

The output shows that the kd command works. This method can be used for all sequences of commands. If we want to use the command frequently, the text that describes the command can be saved to a file with the extensions .m. For example, Save[``kd.m'',kd] is a possibility. When required, the file can be loaded by <<`kd' if the file is saved under the name kd.m. Depending on the operating system, the path to the file may have to be given. After loading, the command can be used as above.

To produce complex programs that contain, for example, decision and repeat structures, one should either consult the Manual [1] or preferably the book by Maeder [3].

Appendix A Installation on PCs

Mathematica is normally delivered on several numbered diskettes. This section describes how to install an executable *Mathematica* program suite. *Mathematica* is available for text- or windows-based user interfaces on many computers, ranging from PCs to mainframes (see Preface); we shall therefore describe the installation for each type of platform. Here we shall describe the MS-DOS installation for text-oriented systems and the MS Windows installation for windows-based systems. Before embarking on the installation, security copies of the *Mathematica* diskettes should be made. Unpack your diskettes and, using the MS-DOS `diskcopy` command, make copies of all the diskettes provided according to the normal of your machine – 3.5 inch or 5.25 inch. Place the first overwrite protected original *Mathematica* diskette in the correct drive, usually `a:` or `b:`. The copy command required for each diskette is:

For Drive `a:` `diskcopy a: a:`
For Drive `b:` `diskcopy b: b:`

If your PC has two identical drives, the command can be altered to:

For two drives: `diskcopy a: b:`

For this the original diskette must be in drive `a:` and the new security diskette in drive `b:`.

Once copies of all the diskettes have been made, the originals should be stored in a safe place.

A.1 Installation under MS-DOS

Place the first diskette in the installation drive; this is drive `a:`. If you wish to install *Mathematica* from drive `b:`, this can be done (simply substitute `b:` for `a:` in the following description). We describe the installation in two associated steps: first comes the required input, then the exact text display shown on the screen is given.

Switch to installation drive
`a:`

Start installation program
```
minstall
```

This is the most important input task. After this input has been given, *Mathematica* version 2.0 displays the following output on the screen:

```
                         MINSTALL

                   MS-DOS 386 Mathematica
                Installation Program Version 2.0

You can use this program both to install Mathematica for the
first time from distribution diskettes, or to reinstall
Mathematica once it is on your hard disk.

To install Mathematica you will need at least 12 megabytes of
free hard disk space.

This installation program has a number of steps.
At each step, it will give a screen of instructions.
You can always quit by pressing ESC.
You can then redo the installation by running this program
again.

Each time there is a question, a default answer is shown in
angle brackets.
If you press ENTER, the default answer is used.
If you give an explicit answer, press ENTER when you have
finished.

Copyright 1988-1991 Wolfram Research, Inc.

Hit Esc to quit or any other key to continue...
```

Follow the instruction to strike any key. The display then changes to:

```
MS-DOS Version

   You must specify whether or not the version of MS-DOS you
   are running is release 3.3 or later.  You can run
   Mathematica under any version of MS-DOS above 3.0.

Are you running MS-DOS version 3.3 or later? <Y>:
```

When a question is asked, an optional response is shown in angled brackets (here <Y>). This option is accepted by pressing the Return key. If you are not very familiar with *Mathematica* and the operating system, you should use this and the other options given. If subsequently alterations need to be made to the installation, this is always possible by invoking the minstall program. The next choice to be made by the user is the selection of a printer. The installation program offers the following selection:

```
Printer Selection.

Printers supported:

0:        No Printer
1:        Postscript
2:        HP Laserjet Series II
3:        Toshiba P series
4:        Epson FX series
5:        IBM Proprinter, Proprinter II, Proprinter XL
6:        IBM Proprinter24, Proprinter24 XL
7:        IBM Quickwriter 5204 and 5202
8:        Epson LQ series printers
9:        Encapsulated Postscript File

   Specify your printer: <1>:
```

The best output quality is obtained by choosing the PostScript printer. If, however, no PostScript printer is connected to the machine, there are two possible choices for graphics:

1. Choose a printer from the list that comes closest to the one actually connected to your machine (usually for dot matrix printers this is the Epson LQ).
2. Select no printer, but print everything to a file using the *Mathematica* Display command. This file can be converted using the MS-DOS Hardcopy command into a printable PostScript file. The file can then either be printed out from another machine connected to a PostScript printer or even still printed out via your machine with the aid of a PostScript interpreter (for example, the public domain program Ghostscript or similar). (The output from a PostScript printer gives the best quality.)

At the end of the installation one must provide the licence number and the password. The display for this appears as:

```
Personalize this copy of Mathematica.

You must now personalize your copy of Mathematica.
The password is on the Temporary License Certificate.

Enter your name              <>:
```

In response to this request it is essential to input the *Mathematica* License Certificate which is to be found in the documentation provided with *Mathematica*. If this information is not given, *Mathematica* is inclined to behave in an unfriendly way, such as by refusing to accept further input when one has prepared large drawings and causing one to have to begin work again with a warm boot.

A.2 Installation under MS-Windows

Installing *Mathematica* under Windows is very simple; we again assume that it is to be installed via drive a:. If drive b: is required, read b: for a:. After starting Windows select File Execute from the Program Manager. The screen will appear as follows:

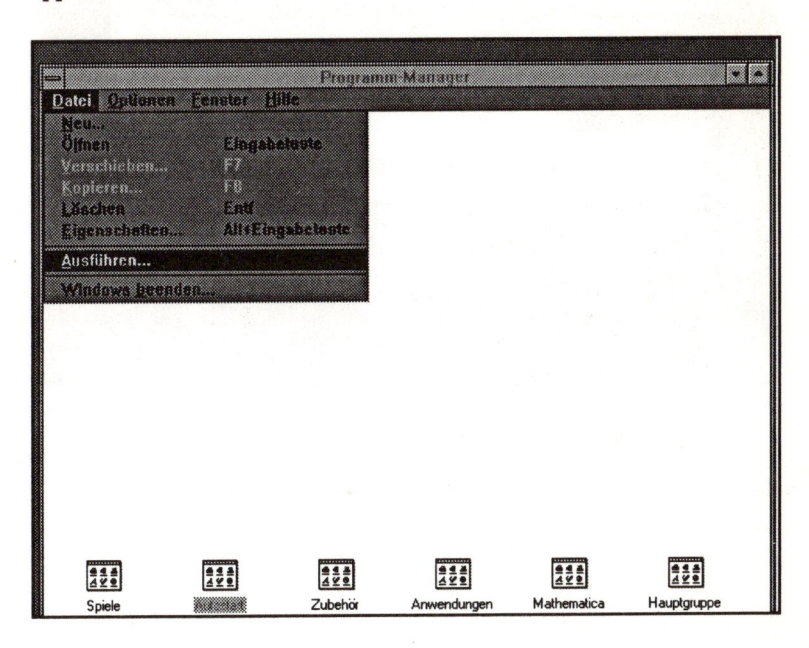

[Screenshot of Programm-Manager window showing the Datei menu open with options: Neu..., Öffnen, Verschieben..., Kopieren..., Löschen, Eigenschaften..., Ausführen..., Windows beenden... Icons at bottom: Spiele, (selected), Zubehör, Anwendungen, Mathematica, Hauptgruppe]

After Execute has been selected, an input window appears, into which we input a:\minstall. After a short loading period the following message appears:

```
Quick  Installation
Custom Installation
```

Select the Quick Installation option with the cursor or mouse. The screen then changes to the following display:

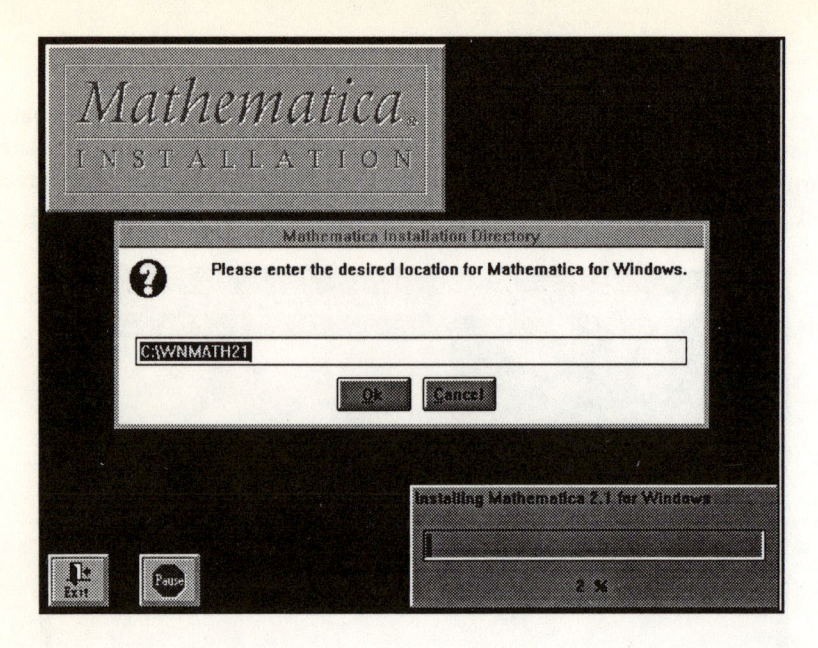

Select the OK option in this and all subsequent displays using the mouse or by striking the Return key. After about half an hour *Mathematica* should be correctly installed on the hard disk. When you first start *Mathematica* you will be asked for your name, the licence number and the password. These should be provided (taken from the *Mathematica* documentation supplied) without fail; if not, *Mathematica* tends to behave in unfriendly ways, such as continually asking for the licence number, before carrying out any further work, or refusing to accept further input after one has prepared large drawings and thus causing the user to have to restart even under Windows 3.1. (Unfortunately this also occasionally occurs when the software has been correctly installed, although not nearly so often!)

Appendix B List of commands

Abs[z]
To calculate the modulus of a complex number or the absolute value of a real number.

Apart[expr]
To separate fractions into partial fractions.

ArcCos[x]
To calculate the inverse cosine.

ArcCot[x]
To calculate the inverse cotangent.

ArcCsc[x]
To calculate the inverse cosecant.

ArcSec[x]
To calculate the inverse secant.

ArcSin[x]
To calculate the inverse sine.

ArcTan[x]
To calculate the inverse tangent.

Arg[z]
To calculate the argument of a complex number.

Array[m,{imax},{jmax}]
Describes a matrix. When a variable is given a vector is obtained and when there are three or more variables a tensor is obtained.

AspectRatio ->...
Establishes the relationship of height and breadth of a graphics object. The default value is 1/GoldenRatio.

AxesLabel -> {xtext, ytext}
Labels the axes. The description must appear within double quotes.

Block[{x, y...}, instructions]
Draws all instructions together. The variables (x, y,...) are local; the commands (instructions) are separated by a semicolon.

Clear[x]
Clears all assignments with respect to a variable x.

Coefficient[expr, var]
Determines the coefficient of the variable *var* in the expression *expr*.

Conjugate[z]
To calculate the complex conjugate of a complex number.

Cos[x]
To calculate the cosine.

Cot[x]
To calculate the cotangent.

CrossProduct[m]
Calculates the cross product of two vectors. To use this command, the VectorAnalysis package must first be loaded.

Csc[x]
To calculate the cosecant.

D[f, var]
Derivative of a function with respect to a variable.

D[f, {var, number}]
Multiple derivative of a function with respect to a variable.

D[f, {var...}]
Partial derivative of a function for one or more variables.

Degree
Conversion factor from radians to degrees.

Denominator[expr]
Provides the denominator of a fraction (rational expression).

Det[m]
Calculates the determinant of a square matrix.

DiagonalMatrix[list]
Defines a diagonal matrix with the diagonal elements of the list.

List of Commands

Display[*output channel, graphic*]
Outputs the graphic (or an echo) on the specified output channel.

DSolve[{*ls == rs...*}, *f[var], var*]
Solves the input differential equation(s) for the required function. The independent variable var must be provided.

Dt[*f*]
Total derivative of a function.

Dt[*f, var*]
Total derivative of a function with respect to a variable.

Eigenvalues[*m*]
Calculates the eigenvalues of a square matrix.

Evaluate[*expr*]
Causes an expression to be evaluated (in diagrams, for example).

Exp[*x*]
To calculate the exponential function (e^x).

Expand[*expr*]
Multiply out and summarise a term.

ExpandAll[*expr*]
Multiplies out the numerator and denominator of a fraction (rational expression).

Exponent[*expr, var*]
Determines the highest exponent of the variable *var* in the expression *expr*.

Factor[*expr, option*]
Factoring of a term. By setting the option **GaussianIntegers->True** complex factors can be obtained. In fractions numerators and denominators are factorised.

FactorInteger[*n*]
Determines the prime factors of the integer *n* with the corresponding exponent.

Frame ->...
Causes the diagram to be framed, according to the option True or False.

FrameLabel->{*xtext, ytext*}
Causes a framed diagram to be labelled. The description must be enclosed between double quotes.

FreeQ[*expr, term*]
Checks whether an expression is contained in a term. If so, the command returns

the value `True`.

IdentityMatrix[n]
Defines the *n* by *n* identity matrix.

Im[z]
To calculate the imaginary part of a complex number.

Integrate[f, var]
Indefinite integral of a function.

Integrate[f, {var, varmin, varmax}]
Definate integral of a function.

Integrate[f, {var1, var1min, var1max}, {var2, var2min, var2max}]
Multiple definite integral of a function.

Inverse[m]
Calculates the inverse of a square matrix.

Limit[term, var -> var0]
Calculates the limit value of a term.

ListPlot[table, option]
Plots the list in a display are. Here the `PlotJoined` option may be used.

Log[x]
To calculate the natural logarithmic function (ln *x*).

Log[b, x]
To calculate the logarithmic function to base *b* ($\log_b x$).

MatrixForm[list]
Displays the list as a two-dimensional field.

Mesh -> False
Emphasises the drawing of the grid background to a 3D graphic. Default setting is `False`.

N[expr]
To calculate decimal approximations. The required number of decimal places can be specified, separated by a comma.

NDSolve[{f, ls == rs...}, f[var,], {var, varmin, varmax}]
Solves the input differential equation(s) numerically within the domain (varmin, varmax).

NIntegrate[*f*, {*var*, *varmin*, *varmax*}]
Calculates numerically the integral of a function. The command can also be used for multiple integrals.

NSolve[*ls == rs*, *var*, *option*]
Solves numerically an equation or a list of equations according to the input solution variables.

Numerator[*expr*]
Provides the numerator of a fraction (rational expression).

ParametricPlot[*list*, {*var*, *varmin*, *varmax*}, *option*]
Plots parameterised curves. The options are the same as for Plot.

ParametricPlot3D[*list*, {*var1*, *var1min*, *var1max*}, {*var2*, *var2min*, *var2max*}]
Plots a parameterised curve or surface or a list of both.

Part[*list*, *i*]
Selects an element from a list.

Part[*list*, {*i*, *j*,...}]
Selects several elements from a list.

Part[*list*, *i*, *j*,...}]
Selects from several planes in a list.

Pi
Mathematica symbol for π.

Plot3D[*f*, {*var1*, *var1min*, *var1max*}, {*var2*, *var2min*, *var2max*}, *option*]
Produces a 3D graphic of a function with two variables. The options are ViewPoint, Mesh and PlotPoints.

Plot [*list*, {*var*, *varmin*, *varmax*}, *option*]
Plots the graph of a function. The options are PlotStyle with PointSize, Thickness, Frame and AxesLabel.

PlotJoined -> True
Joins the points on a graph plotted by ListPlot. Default is True.

PlotPoints -> *number*
Specifies the number of plot points for the curves.

PlotStyle ->
Sets the plotting mode. Options are PointSize and Thickness.

PointSize[r]
Sets the point size for the PlotStyle. *r* is always a fraction of the plot size.

Print[expr1, expr2,...]
Prints the expression (*expr1* ...). String constants must be enclosed between double quotes.

Product[term, {var, varmin, varmax}]
Calculates the final product.

Protect[command]
Protects a command from being overwritten.

Re[z]
To calculate the real part of a complex number.

ReadList["file", datatype]
Reads from a file data of a determined data type (e.g. integer, real, etc.). If the option datatype is not input, the contents of the file are given as a list.

Reduce[ls == rs, var, option]
Solves an equation or a list of equations for the declared solution variables, subject to secondary conditions. With option **VerifySolutions -> True** the test is automatically carried out.

Roots[ls == rs, var, option]
Solves one equation only for the declared solution variable.

Save["filename", expr1, expr2, ...]
Saves the expression (*expr1* ...) to the file (filename). If the file is already present, the saved data is added to it.

Sec[x]
To calculate the secant function (sec *x*).

Series[f, {var, var0, varh}]
Calculates the power series of function *f* at the location *var0* up to the highest power *varh*.

Short[expr, n]
Short representation of a term. Using the *n* option allows the number of output lines to be specified.

Show[graphics, option]
Displays the graphic or a list of graphics. The options are as for simple graphics.

List of Commands

Simplify[*expr*]
To simplify terms.

Sin[*x*]
To calculate the sine function sin *x*.

Solve[*ls == rs, var, option*]
Solves an equation or a list of equations for the declared solution variables. The **VerifySolutions -> True** option automatically carries out the test.

Sqrt[*x*]
To calculate the square root of *x*.

Sum[*term, {var, varmin, varmax, dx}*]
Calculates the final sum.

Table[*expr, {x, xmin, xmax, dx}*]
Produces a table for the variable *x*. If a table for several variables is required, a list of variables can be given, in which each variable is to be described as above.

TableForm[*list*]
Sets a list as a table.

Tan[*x*]
To calculate the tangent function.

Thickness[*r*]
Sets the line thickness under the **PlotStyle** option. *r* is a section of the plot size.

Together[*expr*]
Summarises fractions.

Transpose[*m*]
Calculates the transpose of a matrix.

Unprotect[*command*]
Allows a command to be overwritten.

ViewPoint -> *{x, y, z}*
To set the viewpoint for a 3D drawing.

Appendix C Solutions

In the solutions, a correct input for *Mathematica* is given, not the mathematical solution.

C.1 Solutions to Chapter 1

1. `FactorInteger[2^45-1]`
2. `Sqrt[17] Sqrt[68]`
3. `Log[335]`
4. `N[%]`
5. `Log[4.2048]`
6. `Sin[135 Degree]`
7. `N[%]`
8. `Re[5-5 I]`
9. `Im[5-5 I]`
10. `Abs[5-5 I]`
11. `Arg[5-5 I]`

C.2 Solutions to Chapter 2

1. `Expand[(x+y-17)(x^2+14 x -37)]`
2. `Coefficient[%,y]`
3. `Exponent[%%,x]`
4. `Factor[3 x^5- 5 x^4-27 x^3 + 45 x^2 -1200 x+2000, GaussianIntegers->True]`
5. `Simplify[(x^2-5x+6)/(x-3)]`

For the remaining problems the following variable is defined:

   `fraction=((x-5)(x+14))/((x+11)(x-17))`

6. `Expand[fraction]`
7. `ExpandAll[fraction]`
8. `Together[%]`
9. `Apart[fraction]`

94

C.3 Solutions to Chapter 3

1. `f[x_]:= x Sin[x]`
2. `table=Table[{x,f[x]},{x,0,2 Pi,Pi/6}]`
3. `Part[table,{5}]`
4. `Part[table,4,2]`

C.4 Solutions to Chapter 4

1. `Solve[15 x^2 -2 x -8==0,x]`
2. `Solve[x^4-4 x^3== 17 x^2+16 x +84,x]`
3. `Solve[Sqrt[x+2]-1==Sqrt[x], x, VerifySolutions->True]`
4. `Solve[2 (Cos[x])^2+3 Cos[x]+1==0,Cos[x]]`
5. `Reduce[a/(x-b)-1==b/(x-a),x]`

C.5 Solutions to Chapter 5

Definitions of the matrices:

```
m1={{1,2,3},{4,5,6},{7,8,9}}
m2={{1,0,1},{0,1,0},{0,1,1}}
```

1. `m1+m2`
2. `m1.m2`
3. `Transpose[m1]`
4. `Det[m2]`
5. `Inverse[m2]`
6. `Solve[{2 x+8 y + 14 z == 178,`
   `        7 x+  y +  4 z == 74,`
   `        4 x+7 y +    z == 77},{x,y,z}]`

C.6 Solutions to Chapter 6

1. `Plot[Sin[x]/x,{x,0.001,2 Pi},`
   `Frame->True,`
   `FrameLabel->{"x-axis","y-axis"},`
   `GridLines->Automatic]`
2. `ParametricPlot[{2 Cos[t],2 Sin[t]},{t,0,Pi}]`
3. `ParametricPlot3D[{2 Cos[u]Cos[t],`
   `     2 Cos[u] Sin[t],2 Sin[u]},`
   `   {t,0,2 Pi}, {u,0,Pi/2}]`

C.7 Solutions to Chapter 7

1. `D[Sin[x] E^(4-x^2),x]`
2. `D[Cos[y] E^(4-x^2),x,y]`
3. `Integrate[Sqrt[x^2-2 x+5],x]`
4. `Integrate[Sqrt[x^2-2 x+5],{x,0,5}]`
5. `N[%]`
6. `DSolve[f'[x]-x^2(f[x])^2==x^2,f[x],x]`

References

[1] Wolfram, Stephen, *Mathematica*: A System for Doing Mathematics by Computer, Second Edition. Addison-Wesley Publishing Co., Redwood City, California 1992

[2] Gray, Theodore W. and Glynn, Jerrt, Exploring Mathematics with *Mathematica*. Addison-Wesley Publishing Co., Redwood City, California 1991

[3] Maeder, Roman, Programming in *Mathematica*. Addison-Wesley Publishing Co., Redwood City, California 1990

[4] Blachman, Nancy, *Mathematica* Quick Reference Version 2. Addison-Wesley Publishing Co., Redwood City, California 1992

[5] Davenport, J.H., Siret, Y., Tournier, E., Computer Algebra. Academic Press, London 1988

[6] Leupold, Wilhelm et al., Lehr- und Übungsbuch Mathematik Band III. VEB Fachbuchverlag, Leipzig 1983

Index

Abs 10–11, 87
Apart 19–20, 87
ArcCos 87
ArcCot 8, 87
ArcCsc 87
ArcSec 87
ArcSin 9, 35, 87
ArcTan 10, 64, 67, 87
Arg 10–11, 87
Array 38, 40, 43, 87
AspectRatio 51, 87
AxesLabel 50, 54, 87

Block 80, 87

Clear 13–14, 88
Coefficient 16–17, 88
Commands
  altering 78–79
  to produce tables 24
  for rational integral terms 17
Complex numbers 9–11, 79, 81, 87–88, 90, 92
Conjugate 10–11, 88
Cos 8–9, 33–36, 51–52, 57, 59, 63, 65, 67, 69, 77–78, 88
Cot 8–9, 88
CrossProduct 44, 88
Csc 8, 88

D 63–65, 88
Degree 9, 88
Denominator 19–20, 88
Derivative 63, 66, 76–78
  higher 64
  partial 66

  total 66
Det 42–43, 88
Determinant 43
DiagonalMatrix 38, 40, 88
Display command 84, 89
Display function 62
Display
  2D 48
  3D 55, 62
DSolve 71–74, 89
Dt 65–66, 89

E 7, 64–65, 68, 71–72
Eigenvalues 42–43, 89
Equations
  differential 71–72, 74–75
  root 31–32, 36, 92
  sum 31–33, 78
  systems 38–47
  trigonometric 33, 35
Evaluate 49, 54, 89
Exp 8, 89
Expand 15–19, 89
ExpandAll 18–20, 31, 89
Exponent 16–17, 89

Factor 17, 19–20, 89
FactorInteger 5, 89
Fractions 4, 6, 9–10, 18–20
  partial 87
  separate 20, 87
  sum 19, 31, 33
Frame 50–51, 54, 89
FrameLabel 51, 89
FreeQ 77, 89
Functions 8, 24–26

98

Index

defining 24–26
trigonometric 8–9, 27, 33–34, 76
variable 25

Graphic displays 48–62

I 9–11, 29–32, 79
IdentityMatrix 38–40, 90
Im 10–11, 90
Imaginary part 11
Installation 82–85
  under MS-DOS 82–85
  under MS-Windows 85
Integral terms 14–17
Integrals 66–68, 91
  determinate 74–75, 90
  improper 67
  indefinite 74, 90
  multiple 90–91
  numerical 68, 91
Integrate 66–70, 72, 80, 90
Inverse 8, 33–35, 43, 87, 90

Label axes 54
Limit 68–69, 71, 90
ListPlot 53–54, 90
Lists 21–23
Log 7–8, 63–65, 67, 69–70, 90
Logarithms 6–8, 51, 70, 90

Matrices 40
  diagonal 40, 80
  identity 90
  unity 9, 90
Matrix addition 43
Matrix inversion 40
Matrix multiplication 40
Matrix transposition 76, 93
MatrixForm 38, 90
Mesh 56–57, 62, 90

N 4, 6–7, 9, 24, 30, 32–33, 67, 90
NIntegrate 68, 91
NDSolve 74, 90

NSolve 30–31, 46, 91
Numerator 19–20, 91

Parameterised curves 51–52, 54, 58, 62, 91
Parameterised surfaces 58–62
ParametricPlot 51–52, 54, 91
ParametricPlot3D 58–62, 91
Part 17, 22–23, 91
Pi 8–10, 15, 24, 48–49, 51–52, 55–57, 59, 91
π 8, 91
Plot 48–49, 51, 54–55, 90
Plot3D 55–57
PlotJoined 53–54, 90–91
PlotPoints 56, 62, 91
PlotStyle 49, 53–54, 91–92
PointJoined 53–54, 90–91
PointSize 53–54, 91–92
Print 80–92
Product 69–71, 92
Programming
  procedural 79–81
  rule-based 76–78
Protect 78–79, 92

Re 10–11, 92
ReadList 53, 92
Real part 11, 92
Reduce 28–29, 36, 44, 46–47, 92
Roots 31, 36, 92

Save 81, 92
Scalar product 44
Sec 8, 64, 92
Series 70–71, 92
Short 15–17, 92
Show 50–51, 54, 57–58, 60, 62, 92–93
Simplify 18, 20, 32, 64, 93
Sin 8, 9, 24–25, 93
Solve 27–36, 47, 89
Sqrt 6–10, 24, 31, 93

Starting *Mathematica* 1–3
Sum 11, 69, 71, 79, 93

Table 23–24, 38, 40, 52, 93
TableForm 23–24, 93
Tables
  format 38
  plot 53, 90
  production of 23–24, 93
Tan, 8–10, 64, 93
Thickness 49, 54, 91–93
Together 19–20, 64, 93
Transpose 39–40, 93

Unprotect 78–79, 93

Values 6
  assignment 13–14, 17, 25–27, 88
  boundary 68–69, 71
  clear 13
  interrogation 14
Vectors 38–40
  addition 43
  calculationg with 43–45
  cross-product of 88
  multiplied by a number 44
  subtract 43
ViewPoint 55, 62, 91, 93